IN THE MAD WATER

*Two Centuries of Adventure and Lunacy
at Niagara Falls*

T. W. Kriner

First Edition

J & J Publishing
Buffalo

Library of Congress Cataloging-in-Publication Data

Kriner, T. W.
    In the mad water : two centuries of adventure and lunacy at Niagara Falls / T. W. Kriner.
    p. illus., map, photos. cm.
    Includes bibliographical references and index.
    ISBN 0-9657245-1-4
    1. Niagara Falls (N.Y. and Ont.)-History. I. Title.
    F127.N8K76 1999
    974.798   99-071803

Library of Congress Catalog Card Number: 99-071803

First Printing 1999.

Produced by:
J & J Publishing
P. O. Box 241
Buffalo, New York 14204-0241 U.S.A.

For Teddy, Mum, and the Old Man.

CONTENTS

1

THE DEPTHS OF WOE

The face of the water, in time, became a wonderful book—a book that was a dead language to the uneducated passenger, but which told its mind to me without reserve, delivering its most cherished secrets as clearly as if it uttered them with a voice. And it was not a book to be read once and thrown aside, for it had a new story to tell every day.

—Mark Twain

The Niagara is not one of the world's great rivers, though in places it is broader than the Mississippi, deeper than the Amazon. The Congo, the Nile, and the Huang He span continents, while the Niagara measures less than forty miles in length. Nonetheless, its rich history and the peculiarities of its geologic formations have brought it some notoriety.

The Niagara is not fed by tributaries in the manner expected of rivers, and does not run from narrow to broad as most rivers do. The volume of water it carries is essentially unchanged from source to mouth. The Niagara never floods—unless ice overflows can be thought of as flooding.

Had geographers discovered the Niagara they would have called it a strait—a natural channel between two large bodies of water. Geographers did not discover the Niagara, however. It was discovered by men who perceived it as a river. To the aboriginal people and the European explorers it looked like a river and was employed by them as a river, so it became a river.

When the French explorers arrived, a weak tribe of Indians who called themselves Je-go-sa-sa populated the region. One group of Je-go-sa-sa lived in a village near present-day Youngstown. This small settlement was known as Onguiaahra, and the villagers went by the same name.

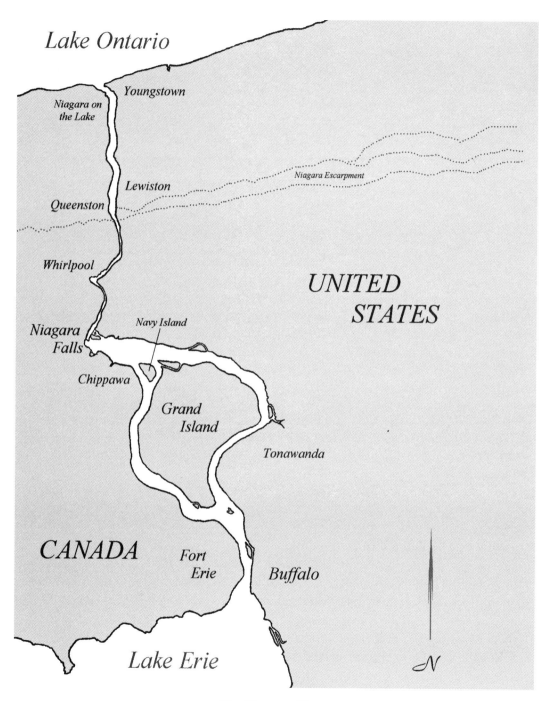

Lake Ontario

Niagara on the Lake

Youngstown

Lewiston

Queenston

Niagara Escarpment

Whirlpool

UNITED STATES

Niagara Falls

Navy Island

Chippawa

Grand Island

Tonawanda

CANADA

Fort Erie

Buffalo

Lake Erie

N

The Niagara River

The Onguiaahras were part of a loose confederation of tribes that included the Tonontates and Kah-Kwahs. They were geographically sandwiched between the eternally bickering Hurons and Senecas. Their precarious existence hinged on the ability to placate their warring cousins. The French named this unfortunate confederation *Neutres* or "Neutrals." By 1700 the Onguiaahras and the rest of the Neutrals had been virtually exterminated by disease and the predations of their neighbors.

The French applied the Onguiaahra name to the river and cataracts near which the tribe had lived, rendering it as "Ongiara" and later "Niagara." There have been scores of spellings and pronunciations of the original name, but only one clear meaning has been recorded: "neck."

Some historians believe the name derives from the neck of land that separates Lake Erie and Lake Ontario. This may be so, but the configuration of the river suggests a different explanation: the Niagara is shaped like a blue heron. Even without maps the Onguiaahras may have envisioned the river as a great bird, with its legs stretching from Lake Erie to the Chippawa Channel and the Tonawanda Channel. The outline of Grand Island forms the imaginary creature's body, and the narrow, crooked stretch of water from Navy Island to Lake Ontario suggests the blue heron's elongated neck. It is against this neck that the Onguiaahras made their home.

The Niagara is navigable from Lake Erie to Navy Island and from the Escarpment to Lake Ontario. These calm stretches of river are used today primarily for fishing and pleasure boating, but in the days of European exploration they were vital routes for transporting military supplies and trade goods. The falls and the great rapids near the midpoint of the river slowed western expansion. Had it not been for these turbulent waters, the French might have explored and claimed the lands from the St. Lawrence River to Wisconsin in a fraction of the time it actually took.

Like the aboriginal peoples before them, the Europeans had to carry their boats and supplies around the falls and rapids. These carrying paths, or *portages*, became vital links to the West. The portages had to be defended from the sometimes hostile Senecas and the intrusive English, so the French built forts to protect them, notably Fort Schlosser above the American Fall, and Fort Niagara at the mouth of the river. When the English arrived they built forts as well, including Fort George and Fort Erie. These strategic outposts were the scenes of many skirmishes until the French and Indian War ended French domination of the region.

Not many years after the French left, the American Revolution began and a new series of battles erupted along the river. The 1783 Treaty of Paris ended the conflict and established the lands east of the river as territory of the United States. The lands west of the river remained in English hands.

When war broke out between the United States and Great Britain in 1812, American forces crossed the Niagara as part of an unsuccessful campaign to seize Canada. Many battles of historic significance resulted, including Queenston Heights, Lundy's Lane, and Chippawa.

The Niagara continued to be an important transportation route long after hostilities and exploration ceased. In the decades following the War of 1812, the upper Niagara became the western terminus of the Erie Canal. This canal permitted the unimpeded movement of supplies and settlers from the eastern seaboard to the Ohio River and the territories beyond. The upper Niagara served as a base for commercial shipping enterprises moving people and goods west. The port of Buffalo sprang up at the western tip of Lake Erie and grew into a large industrial city by the end of the nineteenth century.

In 1855, a suspension bridge across the Niagara Gorge was completed. It brought rail traffic that spurred the rapid growth of industry and tourism along the river. The span was the brainchild of John Roebling, the engineer who would later design the Brooklyn Bridge.

Hydraulic power came into use on the Niagara in the eighteenth century, but it was limited to small milling enterprises. By 1900, however, great hydroelectric plants had sprouted on both sides of the Niagara to supply power to burgeoning chemical and manufacturing industries. Construction of hydraulic canals and weirs to direct water into these plants brought even more commercial activity to the river.

The Niagara has always been dangerous. Boating accidents and drowning here have claimed an untold number of lives. Fortunately, the Niagara has been spared the great ship explosions and fires that have killed hundreds in horrific incidents on the Mississippi, the Hudson, and elsewhere. But like any bustling river, the Niagara has many tragic stories to tell—some of them bizarre.

In 1894 a man disappeared without a trace from a train traveling from St. Thomas, Ontario, to Syracuse, New York. His body surfaced in the Niagara River near Lewiston seven months later. Somehow he had fallen from the train as it passed over the International Bridge at Buffalo.

In 1947 a seagull attacked a young boy who had climbed too near a nest tucked among the girders of the great arch of the South Grand Island Bridge. The boy lost his handhold trying to defend himself, and plummeted to his death in the river.

In 1971, two men decided to scuba dive near the New York State Power Authority water intakes opposite Navy Island. They died when the treacherous currents there sucked them into the underground conduits that divert water to the power plant reservoir in Lewiston, more than four miles away.

These tragedies, while odd, are those that might be found in the history of any river. They are not typical Niagara tragedies, however. The death and mayhem that distinguishes the Niagara from other rivers occur in a six-mile stretch of water that may best be described as *hungry*.

Twenty-two miles north of Lake Erie, Goat Island splits the upper Niagara into two channels of rapids. Newspaper reporters in the last century called the beginning of these rapids the "Deadline." It is an apt name. Even today, any boater unfortunate enough to pass from the broad, calm river above the Deadline into the churning water below it is unlikely to survive.

It is at the Deadline that the river takes a modest downhill turn, dropping some sixty feet in half a mile. This slope is sufficient to turn the river into a seething hell of white water. As it tumbles downhill, the river accelerates to nearly twenty-five miles per hour, then plunges into an ancient gorge over three distinct cataracts known collectively as Niagara Falls.

Luna is the smallest of the three waterfalls at Niagara. Situated between the northern edge of Goat Island and the southern edge of tiny Luna Island, it is scarcely ninety feet across at its brink. The water just above Luna is smooth and swift, but no more than two or three feet deep.

The American Fall stretches eight hundred feet from the northern edge of Luna Island to the rocky shore at Prospect Point. The water at the brink of this fall is shallow, ranging in depth from a few inches to no more than three feet at peak flow. The current exceeds twenty miles per hour in places.

The vertical drop from the surface of the river above Luna Fall and the American Fall to the surface of the river in the gorge is about one hundred eighty feet. Approximately three hundred tons of water pass over their brinks each second. The erosive force of this incessant flood has caused the falls to recede ever southward through a series of collapses in the face of the rock beneath the torrent. Still, the force is not sufficient to clear away the rubble from these collapses. Over the centuries a slope of rocky debris, or talus, has built up below the falls.

At several points the talus extends more than one hundred feet above the surface of the lower river. At Prospect Point the river drops unobstructed for only about forty feet before bounding spectacularly off a rock shelf just above the talus. The greatest uninterrupted fall of water here is no more than one hundred twenty feet.

The Horseshoe Fall, located between Table Rock and Terrapin Point, dwarfs Luna and the American Fall. This monstrous cataract has a serpentine crest line measuring nearly half a mile, and pours about two thousand seven hundred tons of water into the gorge each second. The depth of the water at the brink of the Horseshoe can exceed fifteen feet.

Most of the water passing over this cataract plunges unimpeded more than one hundred seventy feet to the lower river. Rock debris has built up along its flanks, especially adjacent to Goat Island, but there is no real talus. The titanic flow of water prevents any significant accumulation of rock.

The waters below the Horseshoe are a boiling cauldron, but they calm as they pass the foot of Goat Island. The river at this point is about eight hundred feet wide and nearly two hundred feet deep. For about two miles beyond the falls, the water is placid, but swift. Then the gorge narrows and the water becomes comparatively shallow, erupting into the Whirlpool Rapids, three quarters of a mile of white water that ranks among the worst in the world.

The rapids empty into the great Whirlpool from which they take their name. The Whirlpool lies at the bottom of a huge circular basin in the gorge, a right angle bend in the river where the gorge walls are more than two hundred feet high and the water nearly as deep. Here the river turns beneath itself in a vortex nearly one thousand feet in diameter.

The Whirlpool empties into the Devil's Hole Rapids—four miles of turbulent water that runs to the end of the gorge at the lip of the Niagara Escarpment. The river beyond the gorge is deep and calm over the remaining seven miles to Lake Ontario.

From the Deadline to the Escarpment, the Niagara River is a remarkably lethal body of water that has claimed as many as five thousand human lives since the Europeans first laid eyes upon it. This part of the river has inspired fear and wonder in all generations.

The Onguiaahras and Senecas kept no written records, so it is impossible to know how often the native people died at the falls or in the rapids. It is not surprising that only anecdotal accounts have survived from the pre-colonial period. Pierre François Xavier de Charlevoix presented one such account in a letter to a friend written in 1721. Charlevoix told an undated story of ten or twelve Outaway warriors chased by a band of Iroquois along the upper Niagara. The Outaways attempted to elude their pursuers by crossing the river in canoes just above the falls. Their flight ended in the gorge.

European colonial records offer few verifiable accounts of death at the falls. Stories of tragic death at Niagara appeared occasionally in early newspapers. On November 20, 1821, for example, the *Buffalo Patriot* reported that a scow with a crew of three left Chippawa and broke up on the rocks in the Canadian Rapids. There were no survivors. The frequency of such reporting increased with the growth of the region's population and the proliferation of newspapers. In the 1840s, stories of death coming out of Niagara became commonplace.

By the middle of the nineteenth century the killing power of Niagara Falls and the Whirlpool Rapids had already seeped into the popular imagination. The vicinity of the falls had by that time been the scene of numerous shocking accidents. A commentary that appeared in the September 20, 1851, edition of the *American Courier* contained this haunting perception of the place:

Reader, do you know of a Great Cataract whose dark waters sweep by your own door—whose wave crests gleam with the foam of death—whose solemn thunders are made up of the wailings of the bereaved and lost? Do you know of a verge which hides the seething vortex of certain destruction from the careless gaze? Do you know of an incense which smiles in the sunbeams, but rests on the oblivious depths of woe? See you no friend or neighbor plunging by? Hear you no shriek—"A MAN OVER THE FALLS?" Are there no whirlpools where the wrecks of those you love, are circling in the remorseless vortex?

Young friend! We call you friend because we are a friend to you. Are you launched upon that "limitless" tide which is swifter and swifter shooting to the *Great Cataract?* Hear you no muttering thunders? See you no wrecks of the young, the brave, and true go plunging ahead? Are you madly reaching for the flowers which live upon that fatal brim? Are you attempting to tread that rainbow pathway which smiles over the chaos of ruin? Do you ever dream of the treacherous character of that current that sweeps beneath you? *Look shoreward!* Mark your speed! Now to your oars, and a soul in the blade! Ah! My young friend, we write sadly. The Great Cataract is black with death, and the Whirlpool is thick with the wrecks of more value than all the wealth of God's Universe. We shout, but you will not hear, and that dull, thrilling boom ever knells the lost. The waters of that Cataract gather from every part of the land. From twenty-five to thirty annually leap down there upon the begrimed rocks or are swallowed in the waves and borne away! Look! Even woman is there, her long tresses mingling darkly with the foam. And they were ALL WARNED.

The overwhelming majority of fatalities at Niagara Falls prior to the 1870s arose from nautical accidents. It was an unusual year in which a handful of duck hunters or fishermen did not plunge over the falls. Boating deaths at Niagara occurred frequently right into the 1930s. In subsequent decades these tragedies became rarities, in part due to the introduction of affordable boat engines and better safety equipment. Boater education, improved rescue techniques, and the deployment of helicopters after World War II all contributed to a dramatic decrease in fatalities.

Since 1962, the coast guard services of Canada and the United States have enforced a ban on small craft navigation within two miles of the falls. This prohibited zone affords rescuers precious time and "breathing room" to recover disabled vessels. The ban has worked well, but not perfectly.

In 1963, an unidentified boat passed over the Horseshoe during a rainstorm. No debris or bodies were ever found. In 1974, two men testing a boat engine disappeared over the Horseshoe when they lost power on the way from Chippawa to the public boat docks in LaSalle. During the night of November 22, 1995, a 66-year old man and a 15-year-old boy died when their boat entered the Canadian Rapids. They were apparently attempting to smuggle contraband liquor and cigarettes.

Hapless boaters are not the only victims of the falls and rapids. Five stunters have died attempting to go over the Horseshoe Fall: two in barrels, one in a cylinder made of truck inner tubes, one in a kayak, and one on a jet ski. Three daredevils have died navigating the Whirlpool Rapids. A funambulist crossing the gorge fell to his death from his tightrope. The stories of clumsy, careless, and foolhardy people who have fallen from the bridges spanning the gorge or into the rapids would fill a thick book. For two centuries, tourists, children, construction workers, and fishermen have stumbled into the capricious waters. Most of them died. The falls have even been used to dispose of unwanted babies and the bodies of murder victims.

A multitude has perished in "this chaos of ruin." Many of the dead were luckless prey of the hungry waters, but most came—and continue to come—willingly to their doom. For two hundred years suicides have come to Niagara Falls to plunge over the cataracts, jump from bridges, and leap from the gorge walls. Some have waded calmly into the Whirlpool Rapids. A few, perhaps dreading lingering death, have shot themselves in the head before reaching the brink of a fall or loosening their grip on bridge railings. By 1900, so many people had killed themselves at Niagara Falls that the place became known as the Suicide's Paradise.

In 1904, author Orrin Dunlap observed that these suicides were motivated by the same forces that bring people to kill themselves the world over:

> The disappointed lover, male and female; people despondent from ill health; those who have met financial reverses; people simply won to death by the fascinating, coaxing waters; people unstrung by religion; people crazed by drink; people crazed by drugs; young and old, rich and poor; heart broken, sorrowing people, and those who feel their lives are no longer useful, but a burden to friends and family, all have a place in Niagara's list of sadness.

The rapids above the falls exert an attracting influence that has been reported by many persons rescued from them. The dizzying precipice beckons. Some people succumb to the attraction of the water, or answer the call of the gorge. These responses to height and water are not peculiar to Niagara. People everywhere and in all ages have killed themselves by drowning or jumping from cliffs and bridges. Humans may have a biological response to these stimuli that overpower their faculties of reason. Perhaps there are vestigial evolutionary inclinations to fly or swim that arise in some individuals when confronted with the falls and the gorge. The water, the altitude, and the distracted mind may combine to produce what might be called a hydracropsychic effect.

"Many persons, when at a great height, feel impelled to cast themselves to the earth," Dr. L. B. Roberts, a specialist in the field of mental illness, said in a 1900 interview. "So it is with people inclined to suicide when gazing at the mad rush of waters at Niagara. They can't resist the influence to hurl themselves into the torrent."

Some of these impulsive suicides, as though awakened from a hypnotic trance, fight to survive as soon as they enter the water. Scores of them have been rescued over the decades. Sadly, most of these spontaneous suicides are successful. Their stories are heart-rending.

What joy could have buoyed the heart of the young man who in 1981 plunged over the Horseshoe and survived? He waded into the water to end his life, yet surfaced below the falls unscathed. Did he take it as a sign from God? As he began to swim did he resolve to live a different, happier life? We will never know. Ten feet from the shore below Table Rock, a powerful undertow sucked him into the depths. What terror passed through his mind as the river whirled him down into the darkness?

In 1986, an unidentified woman leaped into the river above the Horseshoe and swam over the brink. She, too, survived the plunge and fought to preserve the life she had only a moment before attempted to destroy. With determined strokes she made her way to the rocks, but she was too exhausted to pull herself to safety or even find a handhold. She vanished before witnesses could summon help.

Willingly, impulsively, or reluctantly, thousands of men and women have killed themselves at Niagara. Over the last several decades Niagara suicides have averaged twelve per year, despite the vigilance of police authorities on both sides of the river. There is nothing to suggest that this average will decline.

The Niagara may not be one of the world's great rivers, despite its undeniable beauty and inexhaustible supply of hydraulic power, but gallon for gallon it may be the world's deadliest. For two centuries the swift green waters of the Niagara River have been nothing less than a chaos of ruin, and the depths of woe.

2

LEAPING LADIES

The beauty, shattered by the laws
That have creation in their keeping,
No longer trembles at applause,
Or over children that are sleeping . . .

—Edwin Arlington Robinson

The expansion of railroads in the 1840s made Niagara a practical destination for sightseers. It also made the great cataracts a terminus for those with more serious intentions. By 1870 "doing the falls" for a vacation or honeymoon had become immensely popular with the wealthy and the working class alike. But as the number of visitors swelled over the decades, so did the ranks of suicides. "Doing the falls" became a fashionable exit from an unpalatable existence for scores of Victorian ladies and gentlemen.

Nineteenth century suicide methods were fairly reliable, though the gas jet, a bullet to the head, or a quaff of carbolic acid could result in ghastly, lingering death. Besides, there was something base—uncouth—about these techniques. Niagara offered an elegant alternative. Now the jilted lover, the failed entrepreneur, and the melancholiac had the assurance of a quick, certain death in a lovely setting—a romantic, poetic death.

By the turn of the century self-murder at Niagara had evolved into ritual: the suicide would arrive by train from New York, Toronto, or Detroit, leave an explanatory note in a conspicuous place, then wade into the hungry green waters above the falls. Some preferred to jump from the bridges spanning the Niagara Gorge; others threw themselves into the abyss from the nearest cliff. Usually the suicides were young and intelligent. More often than not they were female.

An illustration from the 1886 story, "Miss Ryler's Suicide at Niagara Falls."
Nineteenth century fiction romanticized death at Niagara.

It is likely that the first women to kill themselves at Niagara were Onguiaahras and Senecas. No doubt the early European settlers lost wives and daughters to the cataracts as well, but there are few documents and scant anecdotal evidence to suggest that suicide at Niagara was anything but a rarity prior to 1800. It remained an uncommon occurrence until the trains brought throngs of people.

In the 1850s North American newspapers began to run stories describing Niagara suicides. The reporters of the day had a fascination with the place—especially when it produced a suicide or a fatal boating mishap. They eagerly described the victims and events in lurid—sometimes embellished—detail, often using secondhand accounts hastily relayed by post or telegraph. In their rush to get these stories into print, they frequently misreported names and dates—even the number of victims. Typical of news accounts of the period is this story from the *New York Herald* of August 8, 1852:

> SUICIDE AT NIAGARA FALLS—A milliner lady, 22 years of age, divested herself of all her clothing and threw herself into the Niagara River, just above the cataract, from whence she was thrown down the mighty fall. She was fished for by the people on the rocks, for an hour without success. The sight was horrible to behold; the body seemed to be tossed upward by an invisible power below, and again it was drawn under from sight. She soon appeared with her limbs up, or some other portion of her body, only to be drawn back by the remorseless power, and after describing a few momentary gyrations, to be tossed again like a cork out of the water. Ropes were thrown a long time with nooses, but without success, for by the time the ropes were thrown for her, she was under water and was distant two rods from the shore, where boats cannot live an instant. Finally, she was secured by a sturgeon spear and brought to shore.

Such grisly description was merely a sample of what was to come. As the frequency of suicide increased over the ensuing decades, so did the quantity of detail in the news accounts. No aspect of the personal lives of the suicides was sacred, and no gruesome particular of their deaths went undescribed.

On November 18, 1870, Margaret Avery, the 45-year-old wife of Chicago lumber merchant T. M. Avery, left her fashionable West Washington Street house at 4:30 p.m., ostensibly to visit an acquaintance and do some shopping. She failed to return home that evening.

T. M. Avery had acquired considerable respect and influence in his city. His wealth made him a conspicuous member of the First Congregational Church. He sat on the Chicago Board of Education. He had two fine sons. His life would have been a happy one had it not been for the tragedy that struck his family twelve years earlier.

In 1858 Margaret Avery contracted typhoid. A lengthy convalescence restored much of her physical health, but her personality was irrevocably altered. It was as though she never fully emerged from her fever. She likely had suffered some form of organic brain syndrome. A woman who, by all accounts, had been outgoing and happy became reclusive and despondent. Her condition worsened so over the years that those closest to her came to be on constant guard for fear that some harm might befall her. The Avery family began to hope for a recovery in 1870 when Margaret seemed to emerge from her melancholy. She started to go out more and even visited old friends. All hope evaporated, however, when she disappeared on Friday, November 18.

Late that evening T. M. Avery began to exert his considerable influence in an effort to get his wife safely home. He imposed upon powerful friends and police officials. In no time more than a thousand uniformed men and citizen volunteers were scouring the city for the missing woman. The following day advertisements offering a reward for her return appeared in the Chicago newspapers.

As the search got underway Margaret Avery was on a Michigan Southern Railroad train bound for Buffalo. The conductor would later recall her as the respectably dressed woman who sat alone muttering to herself. In the afternoon of November 19, she arrived at Niagara Falls, New York, and took a room at the Spencer House. She signed the hotel register as "Mrs. Hill" of Chicago.

Early Sunday morning she took breakfast at the hotel. None of the other guests or hotel staff noticed anything unusual about her behavior. After the meal she returned to her room and remained there for more than an hour. At about 9:30 she stopped at the hotel office and asked for directions to the falls. A married couple happened to be there at that time and offered her a ride. Margaret declined, explaining that she wanted to walk and spend some time alone.

Shortly after 10:00, she reached the Goat Island Bridge and slowly crossed it to Bath Island. Then she returned to the middle of the span and stood along the iron railing. She stared down into the rapids for a moment then began to pace.

John Dutcher, the bridge gatekeeper, saw her walking back and forth. He thought it a bit odd because it was such a damp, cold morning, but it never occurred to him that her behavior was a prelude to suicide. She seemed to be waiting for someone or perhaps trying to decide where to go. She paced almost continuously for an hour, then stopped abruptly and climbed over the railing. She stood with her feet on a lip on the outside face of the bridge with a tight grip on the handrail.

Dutcher shouted and ran toward her. He was within forty feet of her when she turned and briefly gazed at him. Then she relaxed her grip and dropped into the rapids. Dutcher could do nothing but watch helplessly as she surged through the torrent. Less than a minute later, she disappeared over the brink of the American Fall.

Even as Margaret Avery foundered in the savage currents of the Niagara River, pastors in Chicago were exhorting their congregations to assist in the search effort. Detectives and patrolmen were combing the city for clues. More than one hundred volunteers dispatched by the Chicago and Northwestern Railroad were en route to Elgin, Illinois to keep watch at the train stations. T. M. Avery waited anxiously for good news.

When Mr. Cluck, the manager of the Spencer House, learned of the suicide he immediately thought of "Mrs. Hill." He remembered that she had asked that morning how to get to the falls, and that she had made a point of traveling alone. When the woman failed to return from her walk, Cluck decided to inspect her room.

He was surprised to find that his guest had no luggage. The only personal items in the room were a purse and two letters: one addressed to T. M. Avery in Chicago, the other to Cluck. The note to Cluck was brief and seemed to confirm that his missing guest was the woman who had gone over the fall. The note directed him to forward the other letter to Mr. Avery in the event "Mrs. Hill" failed to return to the Spencer House that day. It also instructed him to pay the hotel bill from the money in her purse. Instead of mailing the letter, Cluck went to the telegraph office and wired T. M. Avery.

Margaret Avery's brother, H. E. Culver, arrived from Chicago the following day. With him came S. M. Moore, a family friend. Upon their arrival they posted a three hundred dollar reward for the recovery of Margaret's body.

On Tuesday, November 22, 1870, a ferryman named William Glassbrook found her battered corpse floating among the rocks along the Canadian shore not far from the Maid of the Mist landing.

Culver and Moore conveyed the body of Margaret Avery to Chicago for burial.

J. J. Schofield was a skilled telegrapher employed in the Toronto office of the Dominion Telegraph Company. She was also a promising young writer whose work had been featured in several magazines. In the summer of 1877 she quit her job after contracting pulmonary tuberculosis. In the preceding twelve months she had lost a sister and two brothers to the dread disease.

When she left her job, she also left her family and fiancé, C. A. Kelly, to relocate to a sanatorium on Staten Island. The move seemed to restore her health, but over the ensuing months an infection settled in her lungs. In the autumn of 1877 she penned an incoherent letter to Kelly in which she expressed her fears that she was deteriorating mentally. Despondent over her failing health, she stated that her friends and family would not see her again, and instructed Kelly to dispose of some of her personal property. Despite the suggestion that she intended suicide, she still planned to return home.

J. J. Schofield took a train from New York City to Niagara Falls, New York, on October 15, 1877. She arrived at 7:15 p.m. and went directly to the depot's telegraph office. There she wired this message to her fiancé in Toronto: "Trains do not connect. Can't get home tonight. Am going crazy." The telegraph operator later remarked that she appeared to be sick. He recalled that she had noticed his concerned gaze and explained that her head ached so badly that it was driving her mad.

In the morning of October 16, a number of tourists noticed a neat pile of personal belongings on one of the flat rocks along the edge of the rapids at Terrapin Point. A local restaurateur named Woolson heard two of his customers talking about the discovery over breakfast. Overcome with curiosity and dread, Woolson went to Goat Island to see if the articles were still there. When he arrived at Terrapin Point he quickly located the rock his customers had described. There he found a pair of black kid gloves, a purse, three books, and a black silk twill dress.

There was no one nearby to whom the articles might belong, so Woolson took them to the gatekeeper at the Goat Island Bridge. The gatekeeper remembered seeing a young woman wearing such a dress, but that had been after seven o'clock the previous night. He recalled that she had said she was an artist and wanted to see the falls bathed in moonlight. Woolson took the items back to his restaurant for a closer examination.

The purse contained some keys, a blouse cuff with a gold button, a canceled Erie Railroad ticket for passage from New York to Niagara Falls, and a hotel receipt dated October 15, in the amount of $4.50. The receipt was from Tifft House, a Buffalo establishment. Two of the books were volumes of children's stories, one inscribed to "Charlie Schofield" and the other to "Willie Schofield." The third book was a collection of poetry by Edgar Allen Poe inscribed to "Tom." Woolson went to the village police to report a probable suicide.

C. H. Symonds, a police representative, was on his way to Buffalo before noon. He brought with him the twill dress. A desk clerk at Tifft House recognized the dress and identified it as belonging to a guest named J. J. Schofield. Symonds collected three trunks the girl had left at the hotel, and returned to Niagara Falls.

That afternoon Richard Livingstone, the bartender at the Cataract House in Niagara Falls, received a lengthy, urgent telegram from Toronto. The wire was from his former assistant, Sam Harmon, and asked Livingstone's help in locating J. J. Schofield. Harmon explained that Miss Schofield was supposed to be staying at a local hotel. He wanted to know which one. Harmon stated further that Miss Schofield was sick and asked Livingstone to report on her condition. He also asked that the bartender convey a message to Miss Schofield to the effect that C. A. Kelly would arrive in

Niagara Falls that evening.

Livingstone visited the desks of nearby hotels. He had every intention of inquiring after J. J. Schofield at every hotel in town, but he quickly heard of Woolson's discovery. Livingstone thought the articles found on the rock might belong to the young lady Harmon sought, so he decided to take a look for himself. When he finally examined the articles, he saw the book inscriptions and learned of the room rented in Buffalo. He immediately wired this news to Harmon.

Harmon and Kelly took the first available train to Niagara Falls and arrived on Tuesday evening. When Kelly was presented with the circumstances and evidence surrounding his fiancee's disappearance, he broke down. It was clear that she was dead—gone over the Horseshoe. Harmon escorted the distraught Kelly back to Toronto the following morning.

J. J. Schofield's family refused to accept the possibility that she had taken her own life. They believed she had fallen into the river after suffering a dizzy spell. Few at the time agreed with their assessment—an accident victim was not likely to abandon the dress she wore, after all. The *Niagara Falls Gazette* wondered: "For what purpose, save that of suicide, did Miss Schofield cross over to Goat Island alone, at night, and seek one of the most exposed and distant points accessible? No woman in a healthy state of mind would choose such a lonely walk as that for pleasure, nor seek such a place to bathe a head that ached never so hard."

J. J. Schofield's body was never found.

Bessie Hickman was a shapely, blue-eyed blonde with a free spirit and plenty of admirers. In 1886 she married Gustave Luders, a Brooklyn composer. Luders gained considerable notoriety when he became the musical director of "The Spider and the Fly," a popular New York stage production.

They were happy for a while, but Gustave's busy theater schedule and Bessie's inclination to drink and socialize soon clashed. The marriage was plagued with arguments almost from the first. They would argue and reconcile, then argue again. Bessie wanted a carefree life of parties and debauchery. Gustave was dedicated to his job.

Not long after the wedding, Bessie abandoned Gustave and headed west. She took up residence in San Francisco and lived a libertine existence at her husband's expense. She occasionally wrote affectionate letters to him. He regularly sent money.

In 1890 Bessie moved to Denver. She began writing letters to Gustave in which she asked him to take her back. Gustave told her to come home.

Toward the end of May 1891, Bessie Luders headed back to New York. She wired

Gustave to let him know that she would be arriving by train on June 2, but she did not tell him which station. Gustave guessed she would be at Grand Central Station, so he waited for her there at the appointed time. When she did not appear after three hours, he began looking for her. He finally found her at the Coleman House, a New York hotel.

Bessie had taken a cab from the Pennsylvania Station and had spent the last hour or two drinking. She criticized him harshly for failing to meet her. He criticized *her* for failing to tell him where to wait. In no time they were arguing in their customary fashion. They had scarcely established an awkward truce when Bessie received a letter from a young Bostonian staying at the Fifth Avenue Hotel. The man had met Bessie on one of the trains coming east and had become one of her many "admirers." Gustave intercepted the letter and read it. He left the Coleman House in a fit of rage.

When he returned that evening Bessie was gone, so he left a note for her indicating that it was for the best that they remain separated. He also left her two hundred and fifty dollars.

Bessie returned from a drinking binge later that night. When she read Gustave's note she became so upset that she summoned a physician. Dr. S. W. Smith soon arrived and calmed her with a morphine injection.

Dr. Smith returned the next morning to check on her and found that she had not slept at all. He also found a bottle of carbolic acid on her dressing case. "What's this?" he asked her.

"Oh, that's something I had here," she responded lamely. "Perhaps you'd better take it away with you."

When Dr. Smith left, Bessie visited Lena Chase, Gustave's sister. Mrs. Chase agreed to help her get back into Gustave's good graces. In a matter of days the Luders were once again living as husband and wife.

The summer passed uneventfully. Bessie seemed to have calmed considerably; she no longer kept late hours or drank to excess. All seemed well, but early in September she began to complain of headaches, sleeplessness, and depression. She visited Dr. Smith again, but found no relief. She began to talk freely of suicide.

Gustave spent as much time as he could with Bessie. Still, "The Spider and the Fly" kept him away from her for days on end. On September 4, 1891, he went to Washington to attend to a business matter.

On September 8, Bessie announced that she was going to meet her husband in Washington. That afternoon she left the house and visited Dr. Smith to pay her bill. She told him she had to get to Grand Central Station quickly and that she did not know when she would be coming back.

Gustave returned home the next day to find that his wife was gone. She had left behind her packed trunk.

Early in the afternoon of September 10, Bessie Luders found herself at Prospect Point. At 2:00 p.m., Walter Haywood, a failed Buffalo canvasser, waded into the rapids from Luna Island and plunged over the American Fall. Word of his suicide reached Bessie only moments later. For nearly two hours more she lingered, sitting on a park bench. At 4:00 p.m., she walked down to the river and splashed into the seething waters some twenty feet from the brink of the American Fall. She left nothing behind by which she could be identified.

Miss Ryler's fictional death misrepresented the ghastly reality of suicide at Niagara.

R. I. Heim, an elderly tourist from Philadelphia, attempted to rescue Bessie. He followed her into the river and managed to grab her by the hand, but she fought him off and dropped into the gorge seconds later. Heim reached safety only after a desperate, exhausting struggle with the rapids.

On September 17, Jack McCloy, the wheelman at the Inclined Railway, was crossing the Suspension Bridge after returning from a visit to Toronto. He looked into the gorge and spotted a body moving downstream from the base of the American Fall. Ferrymen William Glassbrook and A. J. Walker brought the body ashore soon after. It was a beautiful young woman with blonde hair and blue eyes—a married woman, judging by the plain gold band on her left ring finger.

When Gustave Luders learned of the suicide and body recovery at the American

Fall, he thought it might be his missing wife. He came to Niagara Falls on September 19, 1891, and confirmed his worst fears.

Bessie Luders was twenty-four years old.

The romantic image of death at Niagara has faded over the many decades that have passed since Margaret Avery, J. J. Schofield, and Bessie Luders killed themselves. The trains that once brought the suicides are gone. The press no longer sensationalizes the sad lives and awful deaths of Niagara suicides. But "doing the falls" did not end with the Victorian Age. Women still bring their terrible burdens of mental illness and broken dreams to the rapids' edge.

They will come so long as the river runs.

3

MISSING MEN

Suicide is always courageous. We call it courage in a soldier merely to face death—say to lead a forlorn hope—although he has a chance of life and a certainty of "glory." But the suicide does more than face death; he incurs it, and with a certainty, not of glory, but of reproach. If that is not courage we must reform our vocabulary.

—*Ambrose Bierce*

The men who come to Niagara to die are of all ages and classes, of all manner of temperament and education. They are sometimes inspired by the examples of their predecessors, and attempt to outdo earlier suicides in the grotesqueness or absurdity of their departures. If one man shoots himself in such a way that his lifeless body tumbles into the rapids, another will wade into the rapids and shoot himself; yet another will then stand outside the railing of a bridge, shoot himself, and plummet into the gorge. When one man "belly flops" into the rapids above the American Fall, the next will plummet from Luna Island to the rocks below with the grace of an Olympic diver.

If there is anything that these men have in common, it may be this: they are failures. Failure to face life's burdens, failure to achieve or maintain wealth, failure to cast off a consuming addiction, failure of faith, failure to accept physical disability, failure to stave off insidious madness—failure of one sort or another has brought thousands of them to seek relief at Niagara. While failure may be the underlying cause of suicide at Niagara, this curious fact remains: most of the men who attempt it succeed.

R. H. Trebor and Edwin Miles, members of Clarke's Female Minstrel Troupe, visited Prospect Park on Saturday, November 11, 1888, during a break from rehearsal. At about 4:00 p.m., they turned away from the American Fall and headed toward a waiting carriage. They walked by a man standing at the stone wall near the brink of the cataract. As they passed him Trebor said to his companion, "I wonder how far a boat could come down those rapids and not go over the falls."

Suddenly the stranger behind them shouted, "Say!"

Trebor and Miles stopped and looked at him.

The man yanked a half-smoked cigar from his mouth and said, "They can't come as far down as I can." He then buttoned up his coat, pulled his hat tightly down on his head, and climbed the wall some ten feet from the brink of the fall. Without hesitation he dove into the rapids and vanished.

Less than an hour later Jack McCloy, the wheelman at the Inclined Railway, used a pike to recover the suicide's battered corpse from the rocks in the gorge. On November 12, the stranger was identified as 24-year-old Charles Campion of Buffalo, an employee of the Lackawanna Railroad.

On July 13, 1891, Mr. and Mrs. Malcolm McMillan of Buffalo visited Niagara Falls. They brought with them 12-year-old Maggie Muir, a family friend. The trio arrived at about 1:00 p.m. and spent the next several hours taking in the scenery. It was a hot day for walking, and Mr. McMillan sought relief in several alcoholic refreshments, though he was known to seek such relief even on cool days. At 5:00 p.m., they rested on a park bench not far from Prospect Point. Just as they sat down a gust of wind blew the hat from Mr. McMillan's head. He was a bit tipsy by this time and failed to seize the hat before the wind carried it toward the river. He shambled after it. A moment later the hat, followed closely by McMillan, disappeared behind a clump of bushes at the edge of the rapids.

Mrs. McMillan didn't think much of her husband's disappearance until workmen at the point began to shout that there was a man in the river. A number of witnesses observed the body float by and drop out of sight over the American Fall. Mrs. McMillan knew that her husband had been drinking, and she had just watched him running and fumbling toward the river after his hat. Naturally, she assumed he had stumbled into the river to be swept to his death. She immediately burst into tears.

Tourists and workmen escorted the distraught woman and little Maggie Muir to the office of Reservation Superintendent Thomas V. Welch. There Mrs. McMillan told the story of how her husband came to fall into the river. Newspaper reporters soon arrived to scribble notes on the latest Niagara tragedy. After listening to the sobbing woman relate the sad affair, the hard-bitten newsmen were wiping their eyes.

As they plied Mrs. McMillan with questions a man worked his way through the crowd that had gathered outside the Superintendent's office. When he entered the room Mrs. McMillan fell silent and a look of indescribable perplexity crossed her face. "Oh, Papa!" she cried suddenly. "Is it you? How did you get out?"

Malcolm McMillan stood equally perplexed before his wife and a score of dumbfounded men. "What are you making such a damned fool of yourself for?" he asked.

McMillan's question was answered in short order, but no one present could account for the body of the man that had passed over the fall.

Skeptical Reservation police officers repeatedly questioned witnesses, but tourists and workmen alike were adamant that a man had gone over the fall. At least one man was of the opinion that the victim was an older man, perhaps in his sixties.

Doubts remained that anyone had gone over the fall until the following afternoon, when A. A. Raymond and Will Sherman arrived by train from Clifton Springs. The two men were searching for E. W. Sherman, Will's father. The elder Sherman had disappeared from his home at 8:00 a.m. on July 13. He was afflicted with a facial cancer and had been depressed since the death of his wife seven years earlier. Twice in the past he had attempted suicide.

Will Sherman and Raymond set about looking for evidence that the elder Sherman had come to Niagara Falls. They soon learned that several people in the vicinity had seen an old man fitting his description. Will Sherman then received a telegram from his family stating that his father had sent a postal money order from Niagara Falls, New York, on July 13. Sherman and Raymond were convinced that the man they sought had gone over the American Fall less than twenty-four hours earlier. No sooner had they come to this conclusion than word reached them that a body had been discovered floating in the Whirlpool.

Raymond and Sherman hurried to Canada and descended to the rocky shore of the Whirlpool. There they confirmed for themselves that the corpse of a man was, indeed, circling in the turbulent waters. The body passed close to shore a number of times—near enough that both men could see it bore a close resemblance to that of the elder Sherman. They had no means to recover the dead man, however. At 9:00 p.m., after hours of watching the body, they abandoned their vigil and found a hotel room.

Early in the morning of July 15, Sherman and Raymond enlisted the help of sympathetic rivermen and returned to the Whirlpool. The body was still there. The rivermen snagged the dead man and hauled him ashore. When Will Sherman examined the corpse he was stupefied: the dead man was a complete stranger. He and Raymond returned home empty-handed.

The unidentified body from the Whirlpool was buried in Drummond Hill Cemetery. E. W. Sherman was never found.

Sometimes the tale of a man gone missing at Niagara is best told by the man himself. Consider this letter written to Charles D. Nichols less than two months after the McMillan-Sherman affair:

Friend Charlie —

By the time you get this letter I shall be no more. You must, of course, know that I have run behind at Salamanca. In fact, I have not been able to make expenses since I went there. You see, old man, I had to wait there more than three weeks for goods, and, of course, it put me behind a good deal. And now that I realize how much I am in debt to B. & L. I see no way for me to make the same good, and I can't and won't face the disgrace of a defaulter.

I have come here with the deliberate intention of committing suicide, and I have a ticket in my pocket now for Niagara Falls. I leave here at 12 o'clock and will go over the falls as soon as I get there. I made a great mistake, Charlie, when I went to work for Baker; it was all out of my line, and now that the end has come and I see nothing but disgrace staring me in the face, I would suffer a thousand deaths before I would be sent up as a thief. I never intended to do wrong, but circumstances were against me, and I am now going to pay for the same with my life. Some, of course, will say that I am crazy, but you know better than that. I am just as cool and collected now as I ever was in my life. I owe Louis some $12.00, but he has plenty of goods in his charge and will no doubt look out for himself. I don't know just how much I am behind with B. &. L., but it must be about $35.00.

Well, old man, don't think worse of me than you can help, for I never meant to do what I have, and I guess I am my own worst enemy. You will, of course, see from the papers that I have done as stated, but I thought I would write you anyway, as you alone can understand why I should take my life. And now, my friend, good bye.

If my body is found I think the following verse would be very appropriate:

Here poor, unfortunate Haywood lies:
Nobody laughs, nobody cries;
Where he's gone and how he fares
Nobody knows and nobody cares.

Yours sincerely,
WALTER HAYWOOD
Buffalo, Sept. 10, 1891.

On the same day he wrote the letter to his friend, Haywood jumped into the rapids off Luna Island and plunged over the American Fall. His body never surfaced.

Peter Schemm was a German-born millionaire who made his fortune in America by brewing beer. He became one of Philadelphia's most prominent citizens, and came to count that city's powerful men among his friends and admirers. He was a jovial man, a good husband, and the proud father of eight daughters and a son.

Schemm enjoyed a happy and prosperous life, but as the years advanced, he developed cataracts in both eyes. By the time he was seventy-four years old, his vision had deteriorated to the point that he could no longer mind the daily affairs of the brewery, so he turned the business over to his son.

Schemm went through the motions of his former life: visiting the brewery every day, stopping for a drink or two at his favorite saloon, dining with his family, walking about the neighborhood. He occasionally complained about his bad vision, though rarely did he mention his fear of going completely blind. That fear brought him to Niagara Falls.

On September 11, 1898, Peter Schemm began the day as he always did, by instructing his chauffeur to drive him to the brewery. Four several hours he toured the heart of his empire, then ordered his driver to take him to the train depot. At noon he arrived at the Reading Terminal and sent his driver home.

That evening, Schemm's family became alarmed when he did not appear at dinner. Peter Schemm was a slave to calendars and schedules. He simply would not miss dinner unless something had happened to him. The family asked for him at the brewery and at his local haunts, without result. The last person to have seen him was his chauffeur. It became clear that Peter Schemm had left Philadelphia by train, but no one could guess where he might have gone.

The family was aware of Peter Schemm's concern about his failing vision. He had gone to great lengths to conceal his fears, yet they had noticed lately that he seemed depressed, and that his nights had often been sleepless. Although he had never mentioned suicide, they began to think he might have gone somewhere to end his life.

Peter Schemm Jr. sought the assistance of Mayor Warwick, one of his father's friends. In short order, the Philadelphia Police Department began to telegraph authorities in cities the elder Schemm had visited over the years, in the hope that someone might have news of him. Before detectives had a chance to telegraph Niagara Falls, New York, the police there wired Philadelphia. They had news of the missing man, but the news was not good.

Peter Schemm had arrived at Niagara Falls at 7:00 p.m. on September 12. He stepped from a Lehigh Valley train at the New York Central Station and walked to the middle of the Upper Steel Arch Bridge. He remained there for a few minutes then returned to the American side and rented a room for the night.

The next morning, he hired a hackman named Henry Hickey and took a leisurely tour of both sides of the river. He went to Goat Island and Table Rock, taking in the sights just as any other tourist would. It was not yet noon when he asked Hickey to stop at the European Hotel on the American side. There Schemm had a drink and returned to the cab. He then instructed Hickey to take him back to Goat Island.

As they approached the Goat Island Bridge, Schemm told Hickey to stop. He explained that he wanted to walk across and meet the hackman on the other side. Hickey dutifully crossed the bridge and waited. After a few minutes Hickey looked back and saw his passenger climbing the railing at the middle of the bridge. Hickey shouted to attract the attention of two nearby Reservation policemen, and pointed at the bridge. The cops saw the man on the bridge and began to run, but before they could reach him he jumped into the American Rapids and disappeared.

Peter Schemm had made no secret of his identity. The hotel registry gave the police his name and address. On Tuesday afternoon, September 13, they wired their counterparts in Philadelphia with news of the suicide.

On Wednesday morning Joseph Wittman, Schemm's son-in-law, came to Niagara Falls with John Murray, a Philadelphia police detective, and William Garrett, a Philadelphia city councilman. They supplied this description of Schemm to the local newspapers:

> Age 74 years; height 5 feet 10½ inches; weight about 210 pounds; top of head bald, with a small fringe of hair at the back; full gray beard and no mustache. Wore a dark suit of clothes, a brown soft hat, and carried a wallet in which was a Masonic emblem and a large sum of money.

Wittman then announced a one thousand dollar reward for the recovery of the body of Peter Schemm. It was by far the largest reward ever offered for the recovery of a falls victim.

As news of the reward spread, hundreds of men converged on the lower Niagara. For nine days the banks of the river from the Whirlpool Rapids to Lake Ontario were lined with fishermen and merchants eager to collect the reward. Men armed with boats, pikes, ropes, gaffs, and field glasses camped out in the gorge and along the lower river. By day they stared at the rushing water, patiently waiting for "the Big One." By night, they held their lanterns aloft and squinted into the darkness. The atmosphere was that of a macabre fishing derby with a year's wages at stake.

On September 24, hearts stopped among river watchers when a torso and a pair of legs surfaced near Queenston. They belonged to someone other than Schemm, however—unusually large feet ruled him out as a candidate for identification. A Canadian undertaker preserved the remains, but they were never identified.

Howard Lake, Fred Preston, and Harry Preston, of Niagara Falls, Ontario, made a pact almost from the moment they learned of the reward. If any of them discovered Schemm's body, they would share the prize money. For twenty-three days the three young men watched the Whirlpool through field glasses or rowed about the maelstrom in a skiff.

In the morning of October 6, 1898, their vigilance bore fruit, when they spotted what appeared to be a corpse bobbing through the Whirlpool. They immediately launched their boat and gave chase. After half an hour of battle with the currents at the mouth of the Whirlpool Rapids, they hooked the body with a pike and hauled the gruesome find ashore. The river had not been gentle with the body, as this description, published in the *Daily Cataract*, confirms:

> It presented a horrible sight. Both feet were off at the ankles, the arms were gone, the flesh was torn from the legs, face, and head, and but the front portion of the scalp remained. Muscles clung to the trunk, and these were badly decomposed.

There would have been no hope to identify the body had not most of the teeth remained intact. The gold-filled molars toward the back of the mouth seemed to match a detailed description provided by Peter Schemm's dentist.

Lake and the Prestons were convinced they had found Schemm's body. They were satisfied with the preliminary identification and were eager to collect the reward. The Schemm family was not so sure, however.

Joseph Wittman had given up all hope of finding his father-in-law and was by this time back in Philadelphia. On October 7, 1898, he returned to Niagara Falls with two family friends and A. S. Stergwald, Peter Schemm's dentist. On October 8, Stergwald examined the body found by Lake and the Prestons. He concluded that it was not that of Peter Schemm. Immediately after the examination, Wittman and his companions returned to Philadelphia.

The dead man found on October 6 was never identified, and Schemm's body never surfaced.

Peter Schemm was not the last man to commit suicide at Niagara in the nineteenth century. He was simply one individual in a seemingly unending list of suicides that continues through the present day. The new century saw new suicides. Year after year, decade after decade, men came to Niagara to end their lives. They still come.

At about 4:00 p.m. on March 8, 1998, a young man wearing a baseball cap and swimming goggles climbed the railing along the rapids in Prospect Park. He waded into the churning water a little more than two hundred feet from the brink of the American Fall. The current swept him off his feet and carried him to his death a moment later.

Park Police investigators began a routine search of the area for clues that might lead to the identity of the suicide. They found and inspected an unattended pickup truck in a Reservation parking area. In the truck they found a map and a note that read, "Check 187 Marine Drive. It's Important." The vehicle belonged to 31-year-old John Bull, a drywall contractor residing in Amherst, New York, at the address mentioned in the note.

Park Police officers were surprised to learn that the address was familiar to their counterparts in Amherst. Police officers there had been summoned to the Bull residence two months earlier to investigate a domestic dispute.

Investigators from both police agencies visited 187 Marine Drive in the evening of March 8. There, in a bedroom, they discovered the corpse of Bull's wife, 26-year-old Sandra Columbo. An autopsy established that the dead woman had been strangled, and that she was more than six months pregnant at the time of her murder.

Bull and Sandra had endured a tempestuous relationship together at their Marine Drive home. In January 1998, Columbo moved out and took up residence with the father of her 2-year-old son, but by mid-February she and Bull had reconciled and were married at Niagara Falls, New York.

John Bull left a lengthy suicide note at the murder scene that established the date and circumstances of his wife's death. On Wednesday, March 4, the couple argued as they had so often before, but this time Bull lost control and killed his wife. Over the next four days he wrestled with his conscience and worked up the nerve to kill himself.

Funeral services for Sandra Lee Mason-Columbo were conducted at St. Mark's Episcopal Church in North Tonawanda on March 12, 1998.

John Bull's body is still missing.

At sunrise on July 9, 1998, another young man jumped into the river, this time above the Horseshoe. Like their American counterparts four months earlier, Canadian park police found an abandoned car. The vehicle's registration led to a visit to the Oshawa home of 38-year-old Jeffrey Williams. In a bedroom of Williams' residence investigating officers from the Durham Regional Police found the corpse of his 32-year-old wife, Leslie. They also found a suicide note.

Jeffrey Williams had apparently murdered his wife of six years by splitting her head open with an ax some two weeks earlier. He stayed in the house for several days after the murder, but the stench of the decomposing body eventually forced him to take a room at a nearby motel. Still, he returned home every day to pick up his mail. Neighbors saw him sitting on the front porch the day before he killed himself.

On the beautiful sunny morning of July 13, the body of Jeffrey Williams surfaced in the Whirlpool.

4

THE FIRECRACKER

One may fall but he falls by himself—
Falls by himself with himself to blame,
One may attain and to him is the pelf,
Loot of the city in Gold or Fame.
Plunder of earth shall be all his own
Who travels the fastest and travels
alone.

—Rudyard Kipling

Niagara has attracted daredevils since 1829, when Sam Patch, a Massachusetts mill worker, gave high-diving exhibitions at the foot of Goat Island. Jean François Gravelet, a French funambulist who billed himself as "Blondin," repeatedly crossed the gorge below the falls on a tightrope in 1859 and again in 1860. Blondin's performances spawned a rope-walking craze that lasted for more than three decades. The fascination with funambulists eventually passed, in part because a new breed of stunters had come to Niagara to challenge the river itself.

In 1882, Captain Matthew Webb drowned attempting to swim the Whirlpool Rapids. In 1886, a Boston police officer named William Kendall successfully swam the rapids wearing a cork life jacket. Carlisle Graham, a Philadelphia cooper, rode one of his own barrels through the rapids in that same year. These successes inspired a series of imitators that included barrel riders, swimmers, and boatmen.

With the rapids conquered, some adventurous spirits looked to the falls as the next challenge. No one seriously considered plunging over the rock-choked American Fall, but the Horseshoe poured into deep water, making it the target of glory-seekers. Three men claimed to have gone over the Horseshoe in the latter decades of the nineteenth century, the first in 1883. All proved to be frauds. Throughout these years prospective daredevils performed experiments with live animals and barrels, but a successful human trip over the Horseshoe did not occur until after the turn of the century. To the surprise and dismay of many, the first person to survive the plunge was not one of the burly men who had long contemplated that honor.

On October 24, 1901, Annie Taylor, a 63-year-old widow from Auburn, New York, rode an oak barrel over the crest of the great fall and survived with only minor injuries. Taylor hoped the stunt would bring her fame and fortune. Although she achieved lasting fame, she never turned her notoriety into cash. She was destitute at the time of her death in 1921.

Over the ensuing ninety-four years, thirteen men and one woman chased Annie Taylor's dream of glory and riches. Their ranks included a barber, a factory laborer, a janitor, a chef, and a Czech immigrant. Two of these daredevils made the trip twice. Just three had training that even remotely prepared them for their stunts: a circus performer, a professional stunt man, and a stock car racer.

Of the fifteen people who challenged the Horseshoe, five perished. Those who survived enjoyed only fleeting celebrity. Just one, Karel Soucek, came close to realizing a fortune. Soucek would have earned more than a quarter of a million dollars in the year following his successful plunge in July 1984, but he died six months later in a re-enactment of his stunt at a thrill show in Houston's Astrodome.

The Horseshoe survivors were lucky. Whether riding in specially designed spheres or carefully crafted barrels, the likelihood of death as a result of structural failure was strong. There were other grim possibilities, as well. George Stathakis suffocated in 1930 when his barrel became trapped behind the fall for sixteen hours. Drowning was always a concern, even for strong swimmers.

In 1990, a 28-year-old Tennessean named Jessie Sharp broke a tradition of falls daredevils. His predecessors had all made the trip in sealed casks or balls. Sharp went over the Horseshoe in a 12-foot kayak. The stunt killed him.

Sharp's rash attempt did not go unnoticed by another young man considering a run at the Horseshoe. Sharp's daring effort fascinated Robert Overacker, a California sports car broker. Overacker had been planning a trip over the Horseshoe for two years at the time of Sharp's death. He had studied the exploits of all the Niagara daredevils and had observed that none of them had attempted to go over the Horseshoe in the open air. He had also correctly observed that most of them had been fools or, at best, shoddy planners. Overacker wanted to be the first to conquer the Horseshoe riding on the *outside* of a vehicle. From the beginning he knew that whatever he rode had to be powerful and fast.

Pat Overacker had given birth to her first child, Robert Douglas Overacker, on July

4, 1956, at St. John's Hospital in Santa Monica, California. Her husband, Ronald, was a professional lifeguard with a Hollywood pedigree; in the 1930s he had delighted audiences as "Baby Leroy," the child star of nine films, including several featuring W. C. Fields.

Bobby Overacker was a precocious child. At the age of two weeks he could turn himself over, and at four months could escape his playpen. He started walking when he was one year old, and began to talk at about the same time. When he was eighteen months old, his vocabulary included such words as "expensive," and "dangerous." By the age of two, Bobby could identify most cars by name. If he did not recognize a passing car, he would announce what he *did* know about it, even if it was only the color.

It was not long before he had a younger brother, John, and a sister, Kathy. As the young family grew, however, Ronnie and Pat Overacker grew apart. They divorced in 1963.

In 1965, Pat married an Ohioan named Jim Zureich. In 1966, she gave birth to her fourth child, Michael Zureich. For a while the family lived in Hacienda Heights, where Bobby developed a taste for speed and thrills. He and John liked to ride their bicycles in the canyon near their home. The land there had been graded in six-foot tiers in preparation for a new housing development. The boys would take their bikes to the top of the construction site and ride down through the mud, leaping from tier to tier, shrieking and giggling with delight all the way to the bottom.

Jim Zureich got along well with his stepchildren, and forged a special relationship with Bobby. He played basketball with him and taught him about firearms and automobiles. As Bobby grew older, he spent countless hours helping Jim rebuild the engines of the family's cars.

Bobby took a driver education course when he was fifteen, and received his California driver's license at sixteen. In 1972, when the family settled in Martinsville, New Jersey, Bobby was dismayed to learn that the license he had worked so hard to earn was not valid unless he was driving a car with California plates. The legal driving age in New Jersey at that time was seventeen. His stepfather's car had California plates, but his mother's Volkswagen bus had New Jersey plates. Jim Zureich took his car to work during the week, so if Bobby wanted to drive in the daytime it would have to be with his mother's Volkswagen. He knew this was illegal, but he did it anyway. In no time at all, he had a citation from the Martinsville Police Department for driving without a valid license. It was the first of dozens of tickets he would receive, most of them for speeding. He became an expert driver by honing his skills on the back roads of rural New Jersey, but he also became marked as the local "speed demon."

"Bob had a lead foot," his mother recalled in a 1998 interview. "He did get a lot of speeding tickets. He was very well known to the Martinsville Police. Thursday nights he spent at night court. I always knew where he was on Thursday nights." As the police came to know her son better, they began to lie in wait for him. They cited him for inconsequential equipment violations—cracked lenses, and the like. Sometimes they would stop him for no reason at all.

Bobby got his own car when he was still sixteen. His stepfather's coworker had a broken down Dodge pickup truck that he was willing to give away to anyone who would haul it off his property. Bobby, who was by this time a skilled mechanic, repaired the truck on the spot and drove it home. At about the same time, his stepfather bought a Triumph TR-3. The car's sleek lines and crisp performance kindled Bobby's lifelong love for British sports cars.

Robert Overacker lived for speed and thrills.

His second car was a Karmann Ghia that he purchased for seventy-five dollars one day, and sold the next for $600 after making a few minor repairs. He didn't realize it at the time, but he had just begun a career as a car broker. It was the only real job he would ever have. He tried delivering newspapers, but quit after several weeks. A summer job as an ice cream truck driver lasted less than two months. He was too independent, too focused on his own goals, to be an employee. Bobby Overacker was a budding entrepreneur who daydreamed of becoming a race car driver.

At eighteen he returned to California to live with his paternal grandmother in Van Nuys. He moved into a room adjacent to her garage and started buying, repairing, and reselling cars. He specialized in British sports cars: Triumphs, MGs, Jaguars, Sunbeams. As the business grew, his grandmother's driveway and lawn took on the appearance of a used car lot. Bobby knew it was time to buy his own home, but he didn't have the cash for a down payment. He hurdled that obstacle by earning $30,000 in a month of frenzied deal making.

Overacker demonstrates his driving skills on a California highway.

Bob Overacker developed a network of friends, family, and business contacts to help him find car sellers and buyers. He was always on the telephone, wheeling and dealing, making connections. He established a reputation for honesty and trustworthiness by keeping his word and meeting his obligations. He often worked sixteen hours a day, seven days a week—to the detriment of personal affairs. His dedication didn't prevent him from finding romance, however. In 1978, he began dating Laurie Ponticelli. They moved in together and ended up living in Camarillo, California. Laurie wanted a normal family life. She loved children and wanted some of her own. Overacker wasn't much interested in children—they didn't fit in with his lust for cars and speed. In the end, Laurie learned to live with his dreams and obsessions. They married in 1991.

Overacker worked hard, but he played hard, too. He liked to hop into a low, sleek automobile and head out onto the freeway with a friend following in a spotter car. There he would drive beneath the trailers of speeding semis while the spotter photographed him. He went white water rafting, dabbled in sky diving, and toyed with paragliders. He even attended a Hollywood stunt school and joined the Screen Actors Guild. Overacker had his sights set on a film career, and actually secured a bit part in an Emilio Estevez film. He wasn't dismayed when his role ended up on the cutting room floor. There would be other movies.

In 1990, Overacker realized one of his dreams when he began driving stock cars at Ventura Raceway. He billed himself as Robert "Firecracker" Overacker, playing up his July Fourth birthday. He was a fierce competitor, but achieved no great success as a driver, perhaps because he was preoccupied with a new dream.

In 1988, Overacker conceived of a stunt that would be more thrilling and dangerous than anything he had ever done. It was a stunt that *no one* had attempted before, a feat he hoped would make him famous: he would go over the Horseshoe Fall on a jet ski.

There was no hurry. Overacker had cars to buy and sell. There were races to be run. He planned the stunt in his spare time, approaching the problem methodically. Getting to the brink of the fall was the easy part, he knew, but landing safely in the churning cauldron of green water below it was another matter. Staying afloat in those vicious currents presented further difficulties. His research began in the public library, where he read about all of Niagara's daredevils to discover what problems they had faced and what mistakes they had made. When he had learned all he needed to know about the history and geology of the Horseshoe, he began looking for equipment.

For more than three years Overacker refined a plan that took advantage of his strengths: he was a good swimmer, a skilled driver, and had trained in paragliding and skydiving. His greatest strength, the one essential to a successful stunt, was sheer nerve. He had plenty of that.

In July 1992, Overacker traveled to Chippawa, Ontario, for his first run at the Horseshoe. With him was an entourage of family and friends to witness the stunt, including his mother and stepfather. He even brought along a two-man motion picture crew to film his ride into history.

Overacker wanted to perform the stunt very early in the morning to avoid the crowds of tourists. He hoped to escape detection, but he was more concerned that his jet ski might land on the deck of one of the Maid of the Mist tour boats that operated below the falls. He wanted glory, but he didn't want to injure or kill anyone.

When Overacker prepared to launch his jet ski near the Dufferin Islands on July 4, he realized that something was wrong. The water level in the rapids was too low—he would never be able to navigate through the exposed rocks. His research had not revealed to him that much of the river's water is diverted to hydroelectric plants during the night.

He took his friends and family out to breakfast while waiting for the river to rise, but when he returned to the launch site for another attempt the place was teeming with sightseers and the tour boats were running. Frustrated and angry with himself, Overacker postponed the stunt until his next birthday.

In 1993, Overacker returned to Niagara for a second attempt. He had tried to convince his old friend Sean Moran to accompany him on the trip, but Moran refused. He wanted nothing to do with the stunt. Moran sent his younger brother in his place. Noel Moran accompanied Overacker, ostensibly to assist in the stunt preparations. His real purpose—apparently conceived by his brother—was to do anything he could to abort the stunt. Overacker had to postpone his attempt once again, this time as a result of mechanical problems with his jet ski. He learned afterward that Noel Moran had sabotaged the engine. Overacker returned to California furious, but undeterred. There would always be another Fourth of July.

Overacker did not try again in 1994, though he did travel to Niagara Falls, Ontario, in an effort to obtain a permit to perform his stunt. He met with George Bailey, the communications director for the Niagara Parks Commission. Bailey listened patiently as Overacker explained what he planned to do. The communications director expressed skepticism about the details of Overacker's plan. He also made it clear that his opinion was of no consequence: the Commission would never authorize such a stunt.

"When I saw him," Bailey recalled a year after their meeting, "I could see that there was something in this man's manner that told me he was going to do it. He had conviction and didn't take it personally when I said he would not be able to get a permit."

Overacker's business kept him from attempting the stunt on his birthday in 1995. He wasn't able to return to Niagara Falls that year until the closing days of September. With a trailer bearing his Kawasaki jet ski in tow, he drove from Camarillo to Niagara Falls in a mobile home. Chris Yeomans, Overacker's business assistant and friend, accompanied him on the trip. Michael Zureich met him there, as did friend and business associate Guido Lorenz.

This time there would be no sabotage or low water. Overacker would begin his approach to the brink of the fall just before noon, when the power plants were not diverting water. His jet ski would not land on the deck of a tour boat below the Horseshoe because his companions would use walkie-talkies to tell him when the boats were clear of the danger zone.

Zureich was enthusiastic. Whatever misgivings he may have had about the stunt were overshadowed by his brother's confidence and determination. In any event, trying to dissuade Overacker would have been like trying to reason with an avalanche. "Bob was going to do what Bob was going to do," Zureich said later.

Preparing the jet ski for the Horseshoe.

On September 30, 1995, Overacker telephoned his mother to tell her the preparations for the stunt were in order. He wanted to know if he should call her again just before he set out on his quest for glory.

"No," she said. "You'll have too much on your mind. I don't want you to be distracted."

Overacker laughed and said, "Well, I'll call you from jail." He fully expected to be arrested and fined for performing the stunt without a permit. The conversation ended a moment later. "I love you, Mom," he said.

"I love you, too, Honey," Pat Zureich said. She made no mention of her concerns. She had every confidence in her son's abilities, but couldn't help worrying about equipment failure.

On October 1, Zureich, Yeomans, Lorenz, and Overacker towed the jet ski to the shore of the upper Niagara near the Dufferin Islands. Overacker wore a self-inflating "Mae West" life jacket, a crash helmet, a red, white, and blue wet suit, and a pair of sneakers. Tucked in a utility belt around his waist were a marker buoy and a hand-held canister containing a 15-minute air supply.

The most important piece of equipment he carried was a parachute pack slung over the life jacket. It was a commercial model designed for low-altitude emergency use by hang glider pilots. The pack utilized a small rocket to deploy the parachute. The only modification Overacker made to the device was to wind a ball of duct tape around the ripcord to make it easier to find and pull.

The jet ski had a large American flag on its nose and the message,"SAVE THE HOMELESS," painted on its side panels. Overacker had always been touched by the plight of the homeless, and liked to hand a dollar or two to the panhandlers he encountered. As early as 1991 he had decided to dedicate his stunt to homelessness, a social problem he thought was grave and deserving of publicity. His stunt had been planned as a quest for personal glory that he would not consider sharing with anyone else, but he did not mind sharing it with what he perceived to be a noble cause. On September 30 he made a publicity video that would be released the following day. For the camera he said, "I think the homeless situation and the way things are happening in this country is something that has to be rectified. I'm going to go out there and give it my best shot, and see if we can make a difference in the United States."

Michael Zureich later expressed the opinion that his brother's enthusiasm for the stunt was divided equally between his thirst for notoriety and his desire to dramatize the plight of disadvantaged Americans.

If all went as planned, Overacker would ride the jet ski over the brink of the Horseshoe, push away from the hurtling machine, and deploy the parachute. Just before he hit the water he would disengage the parachute by means of "quick release" shoulder straps so he would not become entangled in its shrouds. Then he would inflate his life jacket and swim ashore.

Just before noon, Zureich and Yeomans left Overacker and headed downriver. Zureich went to Table Rock and rode the elevator down to the observation deck at the foot of the Horseshoe. He wore a plastic poncho—standard tourist issue—and had a 35mm camera in hand to photograph his brother as he came over the brink. Yeomans selected an advantageous position along the gorge rim to film the stunt.

At noon Overacker received word that the tour boats in the gorge were clear of his drop zone. He powered the Kawasaki out into the Canadian Rapids and accelerated toward the Horseshoe.

Zureich was sitting on the observation deck railing with his camera when Overacker shot over the brink almost directly above him. Zureich knew immediately that something was wrong. The jet ski fell away beneath his brother, and a split second later the parachute deployed, but it didn't open properly—it "Roman candle" into an immense streamer that did nothing to slow his descent.

Zureich watched in horror as his brother plummeted into the billowing cloud of mist shrouding the base of the fall. He threw down his camera and tore off his poncho, then slipped over the railing onto the slippery rocks along the water's edge.

The battered jet ski floats downstream.

Overacker in the cauldron.

Yeomans had Overacker in his viewfinder when the stunt went awry. "Oh, my God," he shouted. "The parachute didn't work!" A moment later he was relieved to see Overacker swimming out of the mist.

Meanwhile, Zureich clambered frantically over the rocks looking for his brother. The battered jet ski floated by him, but there was no sign of its rider. By this time a throng of tourists had gathered on the observation deck.

"I couldn't see him anywhere," Zureich said afterward. "I kept looking up to the crowd, and they were all pointing, and I looked where they were pointing, but I couldn't find him." He finally gave up the search and climbed back to the observation deck. He retrieved his camera and pushed his way through the crowd to the elevator. When the elevator doors opened, he stepped into the car just as the operator was moving to step out.

"Did you hear?" the young man said breathlessly. "Some guy just went over the falls in a boat or something!"

"Yeah, I heard that," Zureich said.

The operator asked him to wait while he went out on the observation deck for a look.

"No," Zureich replied. "I'm in a hurry."

"Oh, okay." The operator seemed disappointed but closed the doors and took the car up to Table Rock. He seemed not to notice that his passenger's clothing was drenched and spattered with mud from crawling among the rocks.

When the elevator doors opened again, a platoon of park police officers barged in and ordered the operator back down to the bottom. Zureich avoided their eyes and walked out into Queen Victoria Park. They hadn't noticed his disheveled appearance, either. When the doors closed behind him he thought, *You Idiots. I walked off the elevator right through you guys.*

Zureich ran to the railing near the brink of the fall and looked into the gorge. "Where is the guy?" he asked repeatedly of the people around him. A number of tourists claimed to have seen Overacker in the water.

"Everybody seemed to think he was fine," Zureich said later. "I was relieved because they said he was swimming downriver." He headed toward the Maid of the Mist landing, encountering Yeomans along the way. Yeomans reported that he had seen Overacker swimming, too.

From the overlook above the landing, they watched a Maid of the Mist boat crew haul Overacker out of the water and lay him on the ground. He wasn't moving. A few minutes later a team of paramedics arrived and loaded him into an ambulance.

Zureich had been hopeful that all was well despite the parachute failure, but now he began to think the worst. He approached a nearby police officer, identified himself, and asked if the man in the ambulance was okay.

The officer responded that he didn't know, but that he didn't think so. He instructed Zureich and Yeomans to accompany him to the station house just across the busy Niagara River Parkway. As they waited for an opportunity to cross, Zureich realized that their progress was not impeded by heavy traffic, but by a road rally. "We had to wait for ten minutes to get across the street while all these Triumph sports cars went driving by." It was a bizarre coincidence—a surreal procession of his brother's favorite automobile. "They were all Triumphs."

When they reached the station house Zureich learned that his brother was at a local hospital. He begged to be taken to see him, but the police instead took him and Yeomans to an interrogation room. They confiscated Zureich's camera and Yeomans' camcorder. The police told them they had no plans to press charges. Their main concern was whether or not there had been more than one person on the rocks or in the water. The police questioned them for what seemed an eternity. Zureich continually interrupted to ask to go to the hospital, but the only answer he received until the questioning ended was, "Sure."

Finally, police officers set up a VCR and produced the cassette from Yeomans' camcorder. Zureich pleaded with them to be careful with the tape—it was the only video record of his brother's stunt. A moment later a breathtaking clip of Overacker's approach to, and plunge over, the Horseshoe ran on the small television the police had provided.

When the video ended, Zureich once again begged to go to the hospital, but the police insisted on running the video again.

"Look, man, that's our only tape," Zureich protested. "I don't want it messed up."

His complaint fell upon deaf ears.

Park police officers eventually escorted Zureich to the hospital. There he learned that his brother had drowned. The river had fooled Yeomans and the scores of tourists who thought they had seen him swimming. The currents below the fall had produced this illusion many times before by flailing the arms of the dead.

The emotionally devastated Zureich was left with the grim task of identifying his brother's body. A grimmer task lay ahead. That afternoon, he called his mother. She answered the telephone on the first ring. All he had the strength to say was, "He didn't make it, Mom."

"Oh, Bobby," Pat Zureich sobbed. "*Oh, Bobby.*"

Michael Zureich, Guido Lorenz, and Chris Yeomans spent that night in the mobile home. They talked for a while, then decided to take another look at Yeomans' videotape. The police had returned the cameras and the cassette after their release. When they played it on their VCR, they quickly realized that it had been altered. To this day, Zureich believes the police intentionally damaged the only tape of his brother's stunt.

"The part with him going over the falls is totally covered over by some spaghetti western now," Zureich said when interviewed in 1998. He thinks the police ruined the tape to insure that it would never inspire other daredevils to try a similar stunt. "I have no doubt that they did it on purpose."

The next day Zureich paid an exorbitant fee to a salvage company to find and recover the badly damaged jet ski. After conferring with Laurie Overacker, he tried to donate it to a local museum, but couldn't find any takers. In the end, he, Lorenz, and Yeomans put it on the trailer and towed it back to California. Laurie later found a home for the star-crossed machine in a museum at Niagara Falls, Ontario.

On October 2, 1995, the Ontario Regional Coroner's Office in Hamilton conducted an autopsy. Azim Velji, M.D., concluded that Robert Overacker's death had resulted from drowning. Despite falling nearly one hundred eighty feet, he had suffered no fractures or other significant trauma.

When Overacker's body was recovered from the water, he still wore his parachute pack. The pack's tether ring, to which the parachute shrouds were secured, had apparently failed at the instant of deployment. It is likely that Overacker had the wind knocked out of him when he slammed into the river. Stunned from the impact, he must have gasped for air and inhaled water. His mother's nightmare of mechanical failure had come true.

Pat Zureich is philosophical about the loss of her eldest child. "My theory is that he was so special that God didn't want to do without him any longer."

Like a meteor that blazes through the night sky, Robert Overacker finally came to rest in the earth near Camarillo, California, on October 9, 1995.

5

DEAD RECKONING

There was an immeasurable distance between the quick and the dead: they did not seem to belong to the same species; and it was strange to think that but a little while before they had spoken and moved and eaten and laughed.

—Somerset Maugham

The human body decomposes more rapidly in water than it does in the open air or in soil. The rate of decomposition depends upon the temperature of the water in which it is immersed. Bacteria and fungi within a corpse feed on the dead tissues and produce gas as a byproduct of digestion. This process is called putrefaction. In warm water it develops rapidly. In cold water it proceeds slowly. As putrefaction progresses, gas accumulates in the body, providing buoyancy that brings it to the surface. This phenomenon inspired law enforcement officials of the mid-nineteenth century to label bodies found on the surface of the water, "floaters." Great numbers of floaters have surfaced in the lower Niagara over the past two centuries.

Floaters are rarely discovered when the river is filled with ice, even in years with many documented accidents and suicides. There are several reasons for this: cold water slows putrefaction, making it unlikely that a body will surface before it reaches Lake Ontario; a body floating in the river in the midst of pack ice is almost impossible to see; the churning ice surely grinds to pulp any bodies that do rise.

In warm weather Niagara's dead become floaters unless trapped among the rocks at the river bottom. These bodies usually surface in three to seven days.

On August 1, 1998, an unidentified man fell into the river at the head of the Whirlpool Rapids as he tried to recover his beer cooler from the water. New York State Park Police searched for him in vain. Investigators assumed that his body would surface, if at all, in the Whirlpool, at Lewiston, or at Youngstown. Strangely, an eddy captured the dead man and whirled him about in the depths for more than a week until putrefaction brought him to the surface near the very spot at which he had drowned. Park Police officers, Niagara Falls firefighters, and Niagara County Sheriff's deputies recovered the body on August 11.

Coroner James Joyce on Celinda Eliza Island with Chief Vincent Iacovitti and Lieutenant Donald Compton of the New York State Park Police.

A floater is unpleasant to behold, even when it has not been damaged by encounters with rocks or scavenger fish. A dark, swollen tongue protrudes from its mouth like a fat sausage. Milky eyes stare from their sockets. More often than not, hair and nails have softened and fallen away. The outer layer of skin has peeled, leaving only a purplish brown dermal layer tinted by burst red blood cells. The body itself, bloated with trapped gases, is a massive caricature of the once living person.

"What you basically look like," says Niagara County Coroner James Joyce, "is a Macey's parade blimp." For more than twenty years Joyce has conducted investigations of river deaths. He has examined scores of bodies recovered from the water.

On a hot summer night in 1983, Joyce, his wife, and a friend dined on the verandah of the Riverside Inn overlooking the lower Niagara at Lewiston. Throughout their meal and after dinner drinks, they gazed out over the beautiful, placid waters. The following morning, Joyce received a telephone call from the United States Coast Guard. Someone had discovered a floater in the river at Lewiston.

Joyce drove back to the Riverside Inn shortly after he received the call. When he arrived, Coast Guard personnel hauled a dead man from the water a short distance from the verandah upon which he had so recently enjoyed a delightful evening.

"Aw, cripe," Joyce remembers saying to himself as the body came ashore. "I was probably sitting here watching the water last night and it was just floating by and I didn't realize it." That blazing hot Sunday is burned into his memory. "They tied a rope to the body and dragged it up by the Riverside Inn, and you know that smell—you know you never forget that smell. We took the person out of the water and his lower extremities, from his knees to his ankles, were almost completely eaten to the bone by the fish. I have no idea what did it, but I can tell you I'll never forget seeing it. I could see the tibia and the fibula—from the knees up it was tissue, but from the knees down it was almost to the bone."

If most rivers treat the dead with rough indifference, the Niagara treats them with outright malice. White water, ghastly vertical drops, and jagged rocks combine to produce injuries not unlike battle trauma: disarticulated joints, gaping lacerations, dismemberment, multiple fractures, decapitation, and disembowelment. The battered remains of what were once human beings then provide a gruesome feast for the river's bottom feeders.

The stench of death is an occupational nuisance for coroners. "It is unimaginable that a human being can smell that bad," Joyce observes. "I think anybody in the profession will tell you that the smell can get to you." He has seen burly cops gag and vomit in the presence of a decomposed body. Joyce long ago adopted a simple technique to keep his breakfast in his stomach. "You learn to breathe through your mouth."

He has seen death in many forms: by disease, burning, industrial mishap, automobile accident, murder, suicide, and medical misadventure. He investigates more than three hundred deaths every year—most of them having nothing to do with the river. This experience has hardened him, to be sure, but the prospect of handling yet another floater is not something he anticipates eagerly. When the Park Police call him to report one, his first thought is likely to be, "Ah, damn."

Joyce's feelings are no doubt similar to those expressed by his predecessors and his counterparts on the Canadian side of the river. No one has ever been enthusiastic about handling floaters—not the coroners, not the firefighters, not the police, and certainly not the occasional civilian volunteer. Still, they do it. Simple human decency requires that someone recover these people to identify them and lay their remains to rest.

As the frequency of Niagara suicides increased in the latter years of the nineteenth century, a minor political crisis developed in Ontario as a result of the many unidentifiable corpses that surfaced in Canadian waters. Then, as now, Niagara's currents deposited most suicides in Canadian territory—usually in the Whirlpool or near the Maid of the Mist landing. The survivors of the dead claimed those that could be identified, but strangers or those so maimed as to be unrecognizable were interred at public expense in pauper's graves.

On March 5, 1900, the solicitor of Niagara Falls, Ontario, wrote this letter to his Mayor and Council:

> Gentlemen:
>
> In regard to the bill presented by Mr. Morse for the interment of a body found in the river below the falls, near the ferry landing, I cannot find any direct authority on the question, but it seems to me unreasonable to suppose that the municipality of the town of Niagara Falls should be compelled to pay for the interment of all bodies cast upon its shores, as, in almost every instance, the bodies are brought downriver and the parties have died elsewhere.
>
> A somewhat similar case as this I believe has happened with the municipality of Stamford, in whose case you no doubt are aware a great many bodies are got in the Whirlpool, and that municipality has generally seen to the expense of burial in case the bodies were not claimed by friends or relatives. The reeve of that township intimated to me not long ago that his council proposed to refuse to pay for the interment of such bodies. It seems to me that the Province should bear the expense of burial in cases of this kind, and I would suggest that this council and that of the township of Stamford represent this question fairly to the Attorney General and have the matter settled definitely, as the Provincial government claim the Chain Reserve all along the river and the cost of the burial of these bodies should be borne by the Provincial government, especially as many of them come from the lake and far up the river.
>
> Yours truly,
> A. F. Crow

The issue was not satisfactorily resolved for many years. Today the State and Provincial social services bureaucracies in New York and Ontario arrange burial of unclaimed bodies.

River deaths have always posed problems for those charged with identifying and disposing of the remains. In 1902, four women were reported missing at Niagara Falls. On September 29 of that year, a young woman's body washed ashore at the American Maid of the Mist landing. The *Niagara Falls Gazette* reported:

Indications were that the body had been in the water some little time, but how long it was hard to determine. It was decomposed to a considerable extent, but around the waist, under the corset, it was in fairly good condition. The features could easily be recognized by anyone who knew the woman in life, but the head was in bad shape. Over the right eye was a severe fracture of the skull, and the head had the appearance of having struck on the rocks or been pounded before the woman entered the river.

Despite a wealth of clues that included shoes and clothing, Coroner Hart Slocum could not identify the woman. She was not any of the four known to be missing. Slocum had her remains consigned to the Potter's Field at Oakwood Cemetery on September 30.

Death investigations in Slocum's time were not unlike those of the present day. Forensic methods have improved dramatically, and the legal procedures have changed somewhat in the past century, but the objectives are unchanged: identify the victim and determine the means and manner of death.

When New York State Park Police find a floater, they secure the body and call James Joyce. When he arrives, Joyce conducts an examination at the scene. Often the body is still in the water, held in place by a length of rope or a gaff. Bodies found in inaccessible areas of the Niagara Gorge are sometimes removed in a Stokes Basket—a wire or fiberglass cage. The Stokes Basket is usually deployed by helicopter, though it can be hauled up the face of the gorge by rope.

Once the body is safely ashore, Joyce pulls on a pair of rubber gloves and begins a physical inspection of the body, taking care not to destroy or contaminate any possible evidence. He notes the approximate age and gender of the victim and makes a rough estimate of the length of time it has been in the water. If the body is clothed, he checks pockets for identifying information. Unfortunately, pants pockets are almost always turned inside out by the savage river currents, so it is unusual to find wallets, keys, or papers of any sort. He uses scissors to cut away clothing in the search for identifying labels or documents, but almost never finds anything of use to him. On rare occasions a pair of tight-fitting jeans will make his job easier by trapping identification in a pocket.

Joyce is thorough. He looks for bracelets, rings, and especially watches. Watchmakers have traditionally inscribed their trademarks on the inside of the watchcases when working on them. The National Watchmakers Association keeps records on every piece its members repair. "If we get a watch that has ever been worked on we can trace down nationally who the watchmaker is and try and ascertain who it belonged to that way." Joyce readily admits that this does not happen often.

"Unfortunately, the watches we buy these days are basically disposable things—when they stop, you throw them away."

The examination proceeds with an inventory of any obvious trauma such as puncture wounds, fractures, or lacerations. He makes note of body features that may help match the body to physical descriptions provided in missing persons reports. "Most of the time we use scars and tattoos," Joyce says. "They hold up pretty good."

Once he has finished his examination, he summons an ambulance. He and the police place the body in a "disaster pouch"—a heavy plastic bag that closes with a zipper. Badly decomposed bodies are usually sealed in two disaster pouches to contain fluids and foul odors.

Handling a floater can be awkward. Disarticulated joints and fractures make them as unwieldy as life-size marionettes. "It's difficult when you put them in a disaster pouch," Joyce says, "because the limbs are just turning 360 degrees—all over the place." Once the body has been sealed, it is transported by ambulance to Niagara Falls Memorial Medical Center.

Investigations at the scene do not always go as planned. On one occasion a Park Police officer slipped among the rocks along the shore and fractured his ankle. The ambulance intended for a floater was instead used to carry the injured man to the hospital.

On another day, Park Police used a helicopter and a Stokes Basket to haul a body from the gorge near Whirlpool State Park. Joyce waited at the gorge rim for the helicopter to bring the body to him. A sizable crowd of tourists had gathered to watch the recovery operation. When the helicopter reached Joyce's position, the pilot realized there was no safe place to land—there were too many trees and no level ground—so he hovered over a grassy knoll and released the Stokes Basket.

"That basket had to fall about forty feet. OOOM, BOOOM!" Joyce chuckles at the recollection—even in his line of work there is room for humor. "Everybody just started screaming. They weren't expecting that."

In all trauma cases Joyce appoints a Coroner's Physician to conduct a post mortem examination, or autopsy. Bodies recovered from the river are, as a rule, trauma victims. For bodies that have not been in the water long, he will arrange autopsies at Niagara Falls Memorial Medical Center. Bodies in an advanced state of decomposition require the special facilities at Erie County Medical Center in Buffalo. He leases autopsy rooms at both hospitals on a per-case basis. Coroner's Physicians are selected from a rotation list of forensic pathologists on staff at Erie County Medical Center through a cooperative arrangement between Erie and Niagara Counties. Joyce's office pays $800 for each autopsy performed at Niagara Falls Memorial Medical Center. The post mortem examinations that require Erie County Medical

Center's autopsy rooms cost $2500. Analyses of tissues and body fluids are performed by the toxicology unit of the Niagara County Sheriff's Department or by the Toxicology Department at Erie County Medical Center

Joyce, Compton, and Iacovitti with a Stokes Basket at the edge of the Canadian Rapids. Ready to assist are paramedics Eric Freischlag and Greg Slussser.

Joyce's investigations do not end with the autopsy reports provided by the Coroner's Physicians, nor do they begin with the discovery of a floater. When a suicide takes place at Niagara Falls, the Park Police obtain medical and dental records from the family of the suspected victim. They provide this information to Joyce in advance to aid him in making an identification should a body surface in the lower river. The police provide him with missing persons lists and other records even as they conduct their own investigation of a known suicide.

As the chief law enforcement officer in the county, Joyce conducts investigations concurrently with the Park Police, the Coast Guard, the FBI, the Sheriff's office, and the Niagara Falls Police Department. He commends the performance of these agencies, but singles out the Park Police for special praise. He uses a single word to describe their dedication, thoroughness, and professionalism: "Wonderful."

It is difficult to obtain clear fingerprints from floaters by rolling their inked fingers on a sheet of paper—the procedure used for living persons. Investigators long ago learned that it is easier to make continuous incisions along the circumference of the fingers and pull the sleeves of flesh from the bones. These sleeves can then be slipped over the gloved fingers of a technician who will ink them and record the prints on paper. On more than one occasion Joyce has mailed "finger sleeves" to the FBI laboratories for analysis, but this technique is not employed as much as it once was. Laser scans and tissue builder injections now substitute for the work of the technician's fingers.

Joyce will do whatever is required to close a case. If the services of a forensic dentist are needed to resolve the identity of a river victim, he will secure them. Poring over missing persons reports, suicide notes, and autopsy results for clues that will lead him to an identification of a floater are routine procedures for him. In the rare case of murder, he refers the evidence he gathers to the appropriate police agency or the District Attorney for further action.

When no one claims a body or the floater's identity cannot be established, Joyce keeps the remains frozen at the morgue for as long as two months before disposing of them. If in that time no new evidence comes to light, he will ask the Niagara County Department of Social Services to arrange interment of the body. These bodies are often buried in pauper's graves at Oakwood Cemetery.

Over the years Joyce has been called upon many times to examine human limbs taken from the river. He handles these grim finds just as he would a complete body, checking missing persons reports, searching for scars and tattoos, arranging autopsies and toxicology tests. These investigations do not often produce results because there are so few clues. Clothing and jewelry rarely remain on severed limbs, though a foot will sometimes still be encased in a shoe or boot, or a finger may bear a ring.

Sometimes Joyce gets lucky. In the morning of August 23, 1981, a boater discovered a left leg floating in the river near Youngstown. Later that day, another boater came upon a right leg in the same stretch of water. Joyce was able to match these limbs to a torso hauled from the Whirlpool on August 22.

On a hot Sunday afternoon in the summer of 1980, Joyce was at his home near Niagara University when he received a telephone call from the Park Police. They had found a human leg and were holding it for him at their administrative offices on Goat Island. Joyce was not happy about getting the call—he and his wife were preparing to take their six children to a family gathering at his parents' house in Tonawanda. Reluctantly, he drove his Volare hatchback to Park Police headquarters.

The leg was complete from the hip joint to the toes, but was badly decomposed. Joyce knew immediately that he had to get it to Erie County Medical Center for autopsy. Rather than disrupt his day further by arranging separate transportation for it, he decided to take it there himself. He and his family were going to Erie County anyway. All he had to do was drop his wife and kids off at his parents' house, deliver the leg to the hospital, then rejoin his family.

Joyce did not have a disaster pouch with him, so the police provided him with a supply of plastic trash bags used for garbage collection. He placed the leg in a bag and sealed it. Then he slipped the leg into a second bag. He wanted to be sure no fluids or odors escaped, so he repeated the process until the leg was cocooned in a dozen plastic bags. When he was satisfied it was properly wrapped, he placed the leg in the storage compartment under the cargo deck in the rear of his car.

When Joyce returned home he found that his wife was not feeling well and had decided to stay home, so he herded the kids into the car and headed for Tonawanda without her. He drove off with three little girls and three little boys crawling all over the cargo deck.

As Joyce headed south on Military Road, one of the kids sniffed and said, "Dad, what smells funny?" He wasn't paying close attention to anything the kids were saying because they were behaving like kids—laughing and shouting and whining and chattering. As they approached Pine Avenue, most of the kids were making noises of disgust and asking, "Dad, what's that *smell*?"

Then *Joyce* smelled it. Despite his thorough bagging effort, the rotten leg had begun to make its presence known. Oh my God, he thought. Oh, no. As he drove, the smell intensified. So did the complaints and questions from the children.

"What is it, Dad?"

"It's just the smell from the factories," Joyce said, but his explanation did not fool them.

"DAD, YOU FARTED!"

Oh, Jesus, Joyce thought. Just let me get to Mom and Dad's. He rolled down the windows to ventilate the car, and slapped his emergency light on the dashboard. Then he accelerated.

By the time he reached his parent's home, the stench was incredible. He pulled up in front of the house and shouted for his parents as he hustled the kids out into the fresh air. He then drove the rest of the way to Erie County Medical Center with his red light flashing and his head stuck out the window.

Not all of Joyce's investigations of Niagara suicides and accidents involve bodies or limbs taken from the water. Many people have ended their lives in plunges from the gorge walls—intentionally and otherwise. Several years ago a casual acquaintance of Joyce died in such a fall. In an apparent attempt to reach the lower river, the man leapt from the parapet wall at the site of the ruined Schoellkopf Power Station near the Rainbow Bridge.

"Just like Superman," Joyce recalls, "he took a running leap and jumped over that stone wall. On the way up he bumped into this tourist. He jumped over the side—never screamed or said a word." The startled tourist stumbled and turned just in time to see the man hurtle into the gorge. Dazed and scarcely able to believe what he had just seen, the man returned with his wife to a waiting tour bus. He was pale and sweating profusely. His wife asked him what was wrong, but he was unable to respond. She thought he was having a heart attack, so when the bus stopped at Prospect Point she sought help from the Park Police. By that time he had recovered sufficiently from his shock to recount what he had seen. The police investigated immediately.

"Sure enough," Joyce says, "they went back and found that this guy didn't quite make the water. He impaled himself on a tree down at the bottom."

Joyce's memory is crowded with images of death and tragedy. "I could tell you funny stories, but if I sit here and reflect on some of the other stories so much," he says "I'd end up in tears."

Despite his professional demeanor and outward coolness, Joyce is touched by the horror he sees. He is never happy to examine a floater or a corpse on the rocks, but he is especially moved when the victim is a child or young adult. He can not help but visualize his own children in such circumstances. Upon coming home after investigating the death of a child he recalls, "The toys and messes and the yelling at kids to pick things up just didn't seem to matter as much as they did before."

"It does get to you," he says. "You know, all life is precious, but it seems that when it's snuffed out at such an early age that it's particularly emotionally jarring."

For more than twenty years James Joyce has been looking into the void, matching Death's vacant stare with his own determined gaze. On call twenty-four hours a day, seven days a week, his professional responsibilities often disrupt his personal life. He has seen and smelled things that he would rather not have seen or smelled. The tasks he is called upon to perform are wearying and often revolting. His salary is nothing to envy. Nonetheless, he does his job without complaint because he knows someone has to do it.

There are not many men who could match Joyce's performance and dedication, perhaps because he sees so clearly what he must do and why his work is vital. He states his purpose with simple eloquence: "At the end of each day I have the satisfaction of knowing I defended and protected the rights and dignity of those who could no longer defend or represent themselves."

6

DUBIOUS CLAIMS

All men are frauds. The only difference between them is that some admit it. I myself deny it.

—*H. L. Mencken*

On July 28, 1886, a ferryman named Pendergast found a man's leg in the lower Niagara near Queenston. His discovery led to a search that produced a badly decomposed body. Mrs. B. B. Crandall of Buffalo swiftly identified the grisly remains as her late husband. The dead man's foot, fortuitously protected by a shoe, bore a scar that she recognized. L. S. Green, the Crandall family physician, also examined the remains. He could find nothing to dispute Mrs. Crandall's identification.

Nearly four months earlier, on April Fools' Day, Bryant B. Crandall had checked into the Western Hotel in Niagara Falls, New York. There he penned a letter to his wife in which he said, "I am sick and tired of life; you will be better off with the insurance money than with me. Goodbye and God bless you." He wrote a similar letter to his brother, then promptly disappeared. On April 8, Reservation police officers found Crandall's hat on the rocky bank above the American Fall.

Mrs. Crandall collected $10,500 in life insurance benefits as a result of her identification, but her new fortune was threatened when William Surret, an old acquaintance of her husband, claimed to have met the deceased on a street in Los Angeles in the autumn of 1886. When the insurance companies received news of Crandall's resurrection, they collaborated to search for him and offered a reward of $1,000 for proof that he still lived. Mrs. Crandall agreed to the insurers' demand that the $8,600 that remained in her possession be placed in a trust fund for three years, pending their investigation of the matter.

A search committee representing the various insurers printed one hundred thousand handbills bearing Crandall's picture and the requirements for securing the reward. They sent the handbills to every Masonic, Templar, and Ancient Order of United Workmen lodge on the west coast. The handbills turned up in police and sheriff offices from San Diego to Vancouver, and as far away as the Sandwich Islands.

Nelson O. Tiffany, the committee chair and secretary of the Masonic Life Association of Western New York, soon received numerous letters and telegrams from persons claiming to have seen Crandall. When the committee increased the reward to $2,000, Tiffany's mail became an avalanche. Crandalls were captured in Portland, Oregon, and Bear Lake, Utah. One poor fellow misidentified as Crandall was held in a Texas jail for three weeks before being released. In all, more than twenty men were arrested on suspicion of being the missing man.

An army of detectives and bounty hunters could find no evidence that Bryant B. Crandall was still alive, so at the end of the prescribed three years, the insurance companies released the $8,600 to Mrs. Crandall.

Despite this apparent resolution of the case, reports continued to trickle in. In 1891, Tiffany got word that Crandall was living in Vermont, but this proved false. Then, in early 1892, he received a letter of inquiry from Mrs. M. Roland of Los Angeles in which she asked whether the reward for Crandall's capture was still in force. Mrs. Roland provided enough convincing evidence of her claim that she knew of Crandall's whereabouts that Tiffany contacted the authorities in Los Angeles. Police officers there found a man by the name of Bryant B. Wilson residing in the Soldiers' Home. Wilson matched Crandall's description, so the police arrested him and held him in jail to await the arrival of police representatives from Buffalo.

In the evening of June 3, 1892, Detectives Lynch and Diehl arrived with their prisoner on the Lake Shore Express at Buffalo's New York Central station. A throng of reporters met them at the train platform.

Bryant B. Wilson limped along between the detectives to a waiting carriage that whisked them off to police headquarters. The assembled newsmen caught only a glimpse of him, and could not be certain that the prisoner was Bryant B. Crandall. They could see only that he was a tall, broad-shouldered old man who walked slowly and supported himself with a cane. He wore a large slouch hat in such a way that it covered his eyes. His head hung down so that only his long white beard could be seen.

Nelson O. Tiffany met Wilson in the office of Buffalo Police Superintendent Morgenstern. He shook hands with the prisoner and said, "Mr. Crandall, don't you remember me—Mr. Tiffany?"

Wilson claimed not to have met him before, and could not recall ever having met the insurance company physician accompanying Tiffany.

"Wouldn't you like to see your boy?" Superintendent Morgenstern asked Wilson.

Crandall's 18-year-old son, John, was waiting outside the office with his cousin and a family friend.

"No. Not tonight, sir," Wilson responded. "I'm too tired and weak. Send him up tomorrow."

The following day, friends and family members positively identified Wilson as Crandall. He acknowledged having lived under the name of Wilson in Los Angeles since November of 1886. When Superintendent Morgenstern asked him if he had ever gotten any of the insurance money from his wife, he said, "No, I never received a cent from her. If I had, I should not have been a pauper in a hospital."

Crandall was subsequently indicted for fraud, but acquitted. His wife and relatives refused to have anything further to do with him. They bought him clothing and paid his train fare back to California. He spent his remaining years in the Soldier's Home in Los Angeles.

Bryant B. Crandall was not the first person to use Niagara Falls to stage a suicide in order to escape an undesirable family life. Numerous individuals had done this since at least 1849. Insurance fraud, too, had inspired "suicide" at Niagara before Crandall's disappearance—most notably in the sensational case of Olivet L. Rowell, who in 1881 nearly made off with $7,000 in life insurance benefits.

Many individuals have attempted to use Niagara as a gateway to new lives, or as a mechanism to obtain insurance money, but some have used the Falls to gain undeserved notoriety.

On July 11, 1886, Carlisle Graham became the first person to successfully navigate the Whirlpool Rapids since Joel Robinson piloted the steamer *Maid of the Mist* from the landing below the Horseshoe Fall to Queenston in 1861. Graham, a cooper, made the trip in one of his own barrels. He repeated the stunt on August 22, 1886, then again on June 15, 1887. Graham became widely known as the Hero of Niagara as a result of his exploits in the lower river, but this modest fame did not satisfy him.

On August 24, 1889, Graham made his fourth trip through the Whirlpool Rapids. Shortly afterward he stated his intention to go over the Horseshoe Fall. On September 1, 1889, Graham and his friends announced that he had done just that at 7:10 that morning. No one at the time questioned that the barrel had made the trip, but several local reporters doubted that Graham had been in it. No one outside of Graham's circle of friends could corroborate his story, after all.

Graham, recuperating at Horne's Saloon, recounted his adventure with gusto. "I felt like a man who has passed into the painless portion of death by drowning," he told reporters. "There was a terrible roar in my ears. I tried to speak aloud in the barrel to break it, but I couldn't." He described his sensations in melodramatic detail, from his trip through the Canadian Rapids to his recovery in the gorge. "I felt a contented resignation," he said.

*Carlisle Graham at the end of his career, photographed
shortly before his last Niagara stunt in September 1901.*

The *Buffalo Evening News* later called the particulars of Graham's account "corroborative detail intended to give artistic verisimilitude to a bold and unconvincing narrative." On September 6, the *News* declared Graham a fake in a front-page headline. One of the paper's reporters had hounded virtually all of Graham's friends and acquaintances until he found someone willing to tell the truth.

A Buffalonian named Frank Haggerty finally confessed to conspiring with Graham's friends. He stated unequivocally that Graham had not gone over the falls. Further, he claimed that not even the empty barrel had made the trip.

It seems that Graham may have had every intention of riding his barrel over the Horseshoe, but not as early as September 1. On August 25, a New York newsboy named Steve Brodie had come to Niagara Falls and announced that *he* would conquer the Horseshoe. Graham, the Hero of Niagara, did not wish to be remembered as the second man to take the plunge, yet he was not prepared to go ahead with his plan on such short notice. He buckled under the pressure of competition and attempted to steal Brodie's thunder. In the end, all he achieved was an indelible blemish on the reputation he had labored hard to attain.

On September 7, Brodie claimed to have gone over the Horseshoe in an inflatable suit manufactured by the Goodyear Rubber Company. Three newspapermen assisted him and attested to his having performed the stunt: W. E. Harding, sports editor of the *Police Gazette* and *New York News*; Ernest Jerauld, sports editor of the *New York Evening Sun*; and John McCarthy of the New York City Press Association. Harding later wrote a lengthy dispatch about Brodie that appeared in newspapers throughout the United States.

Brodie recovered from his adventure in a Canadian hotel. From his bed he breathlessly detailed his adventure for local reporters. He proved to be as melodramatic as Graham:

> When I was out about ten feet and felt myself going downstream so rapidly, I showed my yellow spots and tried to pull for the shore, but it was no use. I seemed to go like a limited express train. I hollered for a rope. I saw I must go and I paddled with all my efforts for midstream. The current seemed to help me, and the last I remember I shot over the center of the Horseshoe Fall, just where the water is the greenest and deepest.
>
> I have a faint recollection of feeling myself going down, striking something, and rising again. When going over, all the sins I had ever committed in my life flashed like lightning through my mind. The next thing memory recalls, I was lying on the rocks vomiting blood, and the boys were rubbing me.

Within days, Brodie and his New York friends were exposed as frauds. Several *Maid of the Mist* crewmen saw Brodie's party more than half a mile downriver from the Horseshoe the night before the stunt, apparently hiding the rubber suit where it would be "recovered" the following morning. If this were not enough, *Maid of the Mist* fireman John Tally watched Brodie emerge from a clump of bushes in the gorge shortly after he supposedly went over the fall. Tally saw Brodie climb into a waiting wagon unaided, where his three companions bundled him in a blanket.

STEVE BRODIE.

The Above is a True Picture of the Way the Above Named Fraud Did Not Go Over the Falls.

Rather than waste a sketch artist's depiction of brodie's purported daredevil stunt, one newspaper editor decided to publish it with a revised caption.

"It is more than likely," the *Buffalo Daily Courier* observed on September 10, "that none of the New York party had even a whiff of Niagara's spray. Such is the truth in regard to the awful and daring plunge of Steve Brodie of New York over the Falls Saturday morning, September 7."

There have always been unscrupulous reporters willing to fabricate stories, but New York seems to have had more than its share of them. The June 29, 1890, Sunday edition of the *New York Times*, for instance, carried a story by Leonard Grover titled, "Over the Falls of Niagara." Grover's piece, previously published in *Brooklyn Life*, was the riveting account of an incredible tragedy that took place near Goat Island ten years earlier.

According to Grover, in September of 1880 a young man named Arthur Midleigh visited Niagara Falls on his way home to England. Midleigh had just ended a brief, unsatisfying career as a cowboy in Wyoming. Desperate to have some great adventure before leaving the New World, he decided to become the first man to row a boat from the United States to Canada through the rapids above the falls.

Midleigh enlisted the aid of Alonzo Gardner, a local guide. Gardner, who had only recently married a beautiful girl named Suzanne, reluctantly agreed to accompany Midleigh in his boat, but only after the Englishman promised him payment of five hundred dollars.

Midleigh's plan seemed plainly idiotic to those familiar with the river above the Horseshoe, yet Grover reports that no one save Gardner's wife tried to talk them out of making the trip. Grover explained:

> No one ever seeks to dissuade anybody from any attempt whatever at Niagara. It is in the air. The natives expect it and it has value in their business.
> If you were to prepare a dynamite gun with the intention of shooting yourself from shore to shore, the Niagarans would simply advertise the fact and placidly see you touch yourself off.

On the appointed day, Midleigh and Gardner climbed into a skiff bedecked with British and American flags. They set out from the American shore above Goat Island with a large crowd cheering them on.

Midleigh and Gardner were both reportedly fine boatmen. Nonetheless, they quickly rowed into trouble. The boat became unmanageable even before they entered the Canadian Rapids. They stubbornly battled the ever-strengthening currents, but soon had to turn about to return to shore. Too far out to reach the mainland, they headed for Goat Island instead, but they were exhausted and could not pull the last few strokes to shore.

As the rapids hurried them toward the brink of the Horseshoe, Midleigh and Gardner leapt to a boulder in the rapids less than one hundred feet from shore. There they remained until the following morning when a crowd of men on the island began preparations for a rescue attempt. A line was thrown to the stranded men, which was used to feed a heavy rope to them. They secured this rope to their boulder and watched as the rescuers prepared another boat.

The rescue attempt was not made until the following morning. The empty boat was sent out along the rope by means of a hawser, but when the rescue vessel neared Midleigh and Gardner, the rapids smashed it into the boulder. It disintegrated immediately and vanished.

Toward the end of the second day, Midleigh attempted to reach shore by holding onto the hawser as men ashore pulled him in. He disappeared almost the instant he entered the water. His head popped above the surface of the river near the brink of the fall a moment later. Then he was gone.

When the sun rose the following morning, thousands of spectators lined the shore of Goat Island. Among them were Gardner's wife and parents. With as many as twenty thousand witnesses at hand, Gardner attempted to reach the shore by the same means tried by Midleigh. Gardner, too weak to hold onto the hawser, was quickly swept to his doom. His body and Midleigh's surfaced in the gorge two days later.

Grover's account of the tragedy concludes with this touching assertion: "Suzanne has twice escaped from her asylum and has each time been found standing on the Tower Rock, gazing wistfully at the rainbow in the mist below." It is a remarkable statement that caps an episode in Niagara history that is as thrilling as the ice bridge tragedy of 1912, the scow rescue of 1918, or the Avery horror of 1853. Unfortunately, Suzanne Gardner never went to an asylum, let alone escaped from one. Like Alonzo Gardner and Arthur Midleigh, Leonard Grover created her out of whole cloth. There are no contemporaneous news accounts of anyone attempting to cross the upper rapids by boat in the latter months of 1889, nor is there any record of two men marooned on a rock. A crowd of twenty thousand did not gather to watch the botched rescue effort. The events described by Leonard Grover simply did not occur. He made them up.

In fairness to Grover, it must be said that he may have intended "Over the Falls of Niagara" as a work of fiction. Still, it was published in the *Times* as history and many readers subsequently accepted the tale as factual.

Newspaper stories spanning two centuries have shocked, saddened, and generally delighted readers with tales of calamity at Niagara Falls. One such story was that of the murder of George Iback, a traveling salesman for the Indianapolis Hotel Register Company. Iback visited Prospect Point on June 9, 1896. As he stood at the brink of the American Fall, a man shoved him into the torrent—or so claimed witness E. E. Henderson of South Bend, Indiana.

The Niagara Falls Police Department conducted a speedy investigation, and concluded that Henderson was none other than the missing Iback. Iback had apparently reported his own "murder" and then vanished for unknown reasons.

1904 was a memorable year in the history of Niagara tragedies. Shocking events in autumn of that year compounded the usual harvest of suicides and unidentified bodies. On October 4, a middle aged woman plunged over the American Fall in what was at first believed to be a case of murder. The body surfaced in the Whirlpool on October 23, and was subsequently identified as Emma Johnson, a Tuscarora Indian.

Mrs. Johnson's husband, Foster, was briefly suspected of murder in the case, but Coroner Hart Slocum concluded there was no evidence of foul play. He ruled the death a suicide.

On the same day that Emma Johnson's body was recovered from the river, another victim surfaced. Two local boys discovered a dead baby in the water near the Canadian Maid of the Mist landing. The infant was a newborn male, and had apparently been alive when cast into the river.

The cases of Emma Johnson and the discarded infant generated front-page stories for the local newspapers through the end of the month. Then, on October 24, a new tragedy came to light. That morning, a Reservation police officer found an envelope on the ground in Prospect Park. The envelope contained a photograph of an attractive young woman, and this unsigned letter:

> Buffalo, Sunday, 2:30 p.m.
> You will never be bothered with me again. I don't blame you for anything, but I always knew right down in my heart that you didn't love me and I should never have tried to make myself believe you did.
> I came from Buffalo to Chicago to meet you, but arriving before your company I learned about your recent marriage and realized then that we were separated for life.
> To me it has all been a beautiful dream and I trust you will receive this my last message of love. I did not address it to the theater, as I know you dislike notoriety, and I am praying that it will be opened only by the one man that has ever held my heart and whose image and voice have been my constant thoughts. You will never know what I have suffered, but I can't blame anyone but myself.
> I cannot live without you, darling. Goodbye, dear, again to you and the world. I hope you will be happy with your new bride and I trust when you are winning other hearts from before the footlights you will once in a while think of poor little "Puss."
>
> P.S.—I have addressed this to the Cheltenham, for I suppose you will stop there as you did last season.

The envelope was addressed to Mr. W. F. Canfield in care of the Cheltenham Hotel in Buffalo. Reservation Superintendent E. H. Perry telephoned the hotel to inquire after Canfield, but learned that no one by that name was staying there. Perry then contacted the Buffalo Police Department for assistance. Canfield, an actor performing with a touring theatrical company, was soon located at Buffalo's Vendome Hotel. He told police investigators that he thought the author of the letter might have been a casual acquaintance of his named Pearl Chester. Miss Chester, it seems, had written several notes to him and had once given him a bouquet of violets. When he saw the photograph that accompanied the letter, however, he denied recognizing the woman.

The Hearst newspapers reported the story in a sensational article headlined, "The Mystery of Niagara Falls." The photograph and a facsimile of the "Puss" letter accompanied the piece. The publicity surrounding the case captured the public imagination. It also attracted the notice of young Lillian Rice of New York City. She saw the newspaper photograph and recognized it as her own. Rice denied knowing Canfield and could offer no explanation as to how her photograph came to be found at Prospect Park.

Police officials in Niagara Falls and Buffalo finally concluded that there had been no suicide. They speculated that the letter and photograph had been planted by a press agent to generate free advertising for Canfield, his theater company, or both. No charges were ever filed in the matter.

For much of the nineteenth century and all of the twentieth, Niagara suicide notes have been viewed with skepticism by police authorities on both sides of the river. Without corroborating evidence a suicide note is virtually meaningless. The best corroborating evidence is, naturally, a witness to the event, but even witnesses have come to be regarded cynically by the police.

At 9:45 p.m. on April 2, 1998, 26-year-old Frank Reading Jr. and 52-year-old Maurice Tinney Jr. reported a suicide to the New York State Park Police. They claimed they had been walking across the Goat Island Bridge in the company of 29-year-old Richard Deloreto, Tinney's former son-in-law.

"I love you guys," Deloreto said, and handed them his wallet and a piece of paper. "I'll see you in Heaven." He then vaulted over the railing into the American Rapids.

The piece of paper proved to be a letter Deloreto had written to his ex-wife. In it he declared his deep love for her and his dismay that their marriage had ended. The letter suggested that his life was no longer worth living.

Park police officers conducted a two-hour search of the shore and tiny islands between the bridge and the American Fall, but did not find Deloreto. A search of the rocks and water below the Fall proved fruitless, as well. They notified their Canadian counterparts to be on the lookout for a body, then called off the search.

The following evening, the police received a telephone call from James Devaney, director of Niagara County Crisis Services. Devaney reported that Deloreto had not killed himself, after all.

That night, Parks Police Lieutenant Donald Compton and Officer Brian Nisbet, accompanied by Devaney, and Niagara Falls Police Officers Stan Wills and John Schuster, visited the home of Maurice Tinney Jr. There they found Richard Deloreto hiding behind a dresser in a bedroom.

Deloreto tried to protect Tinney and Reading by claiming that he had, indeed, jumped from the bridge, but had hung on to the railing out of sight until they left. Tinney and Reading, however, admitted under police questioning that they had been part of the fraud.

Deloreto wanted to adopt a false identity with dyed hair and a new Social Security number after his "suicide." His object was to avoid paying child support.

Tinney and Reading were charged with obstructing government administration and falsely reporting an incident. Deloreto was delivered to Niagara Falls Memorial Medical Center for psychiatric evaluation.

7

THE MAELSTROM

Here the vast bed of waters, seamed and scarred into a thousand conflicting channels, burst suddenly into phrensied convulsion—heaving, boiling, hissing—gyrating in gigantic and innumerable vortices, and all whirling and plunging to the eastward with a rapidity which water never elsewhere assumes, except in precipitous descents.

—*Edgar Allen Poe*

Before the construction of the great hydroelectric stations at Niagara, more than 6,200 tons of water spewed unimpeded over the falls each second. Today, a system of weirs, canals, and tunnels above the falls diverts half of the river's flow to four power plants. Two of these plants, antiquated stations situated immediately adjacent to the falls, use little water and produce comparatively little electricity. Most of the diverted water goes to the Sir Adam Beck and Robert Moses power plants that bracket the gorge at the Devil's Hole Rapids six miles downriver. These steel and concrete monstrosities discharge about three thousand tons of water per second.

The diversion of water above the falls has been a mixed blessing. The inexpensive electricity generated by Niagara's turbines has been a great boon to Canada and the United States, powering homes and businesses in much of the northeastern region of the continent. With the erosive flow of the river reduced by half, the geological recession of the falls has slowed considerably, ensuring the scenic beauty of the cataracts for generations yet unborn.

But the diversion has stolen much of Niagara's aesthetic thunder. One can only imagine the splendor of the falls with twice the volume of water roaring over their brinks. The Whirlpool Rapids are still impressive, but they are not the wild torrent they once were. The Whirlpool itself is now a shadow of the former maelstrom of the same name.

Despite human intervention, the Niagara Gorge contains a hellish stretch of river. The Whirlpool Rapids, once unimaginably horrid, are still among the most dangerous in the world. They begin a little over two miles below the falls and run for three quarters of a mile, emptying into the Whirlpool. The rapids are deep as white water goes, but shallow compared to the rest of the lower river. The water here reaches depths of no more than forty feet, but hurtles along at thirty miles per hour. The great waves of the Whirlpool Rapids sometimes measure twenty-five feet from trough to crest.

In its version of the "International Scale of River Difficulty," the American Whitewater Affiliation, an organization catering to the safety and education needs of canoeists and kayakers, rates Niagara's rapids as Class V and VI, the most challenging of "runnable" rapids:

> **Class V:** Expert. Extremely long, obstructed, or very violent rapids which expose a paddler to above average endangerment. Drops may contain large, unavoidable waves and holes or steep, congested chutes with complex, demanding routes. Rapids may continue for long distances between pools, demanding a high level of fitness. What eddies exist may be small, turbulent, or difficult to reach. At the high end of the scale, several of these factors may be combined. Scouting is mandatory but often difficult. Swims are dangerous, and rescue is difficult even for experts. A very reliable Eskimo roll, proper equipment, extensive experience, and practiced rescue skills are essential for survival.

> **Class VI:** Extreme. One grade more difficult than Class V. These runs often exemplify the extremes of difficulty, unpredictability and danger. The consequences of errors are very severe and rescue may be impossible. For teams of experts only, at favorable water levels, after close personal inspection and taking all precautions. This class does not represent drops thought to be unrunnable, but may include rapids which are only occasionally run.

The Whirlpool Rapids have rarely been run in recent decades. The state and provincial governments no longer permit boaters to navigate the waters between the falls and the mouth of the Devil's Hole Rapids. The only exceptions to this prohibition are the Maid of the Mist tour boats and the Whirlpool Jet Boats, although television and film productions have sometimes secured special permission to operate small craft in these waters. The basis for the prohibition is simple: the currents here are deadly.

The rapids have been the scene of many adventures and tragedies for at least two centuries, and the Whirlpool has always functioned as a sort of limbo—a place where the river dead surface to offer the world one last view of themselves before disappearing forever. One of the earliest records of tragedy on the lower Niagara appeared in the *Daily Albany Argus* on June 26, 1841:

DESERTERS DROWNED

The Commercial Advertiser of Wednesday states desertions are said to be very frequent at the Falls on the Canada side. One night last week 9 soldiers attempted to swim across the river a little below the Ferry. Two of them succeeded in breasting the mighty torrent—the remaining seven were drowned, and four of their naked bodies are now floating about in the Whirlpool. Our informant says they present a horrible sight, tossed about by the mad waters. They are lying prone upon the surface, with limbs extended as if in the act of swimming, and it is difficult to believe they are not alive.

An unidentified kayaker in the Whirlpool Rapids, October 14, 1981.

The Whirlpool Rapids subsequently claimed enough ferrymen, clumsy tourists, and fishermen that the waters came to be viewed with dread. It was not until 1861 that human beings traversed them without dying. In that year Captain Joel Robinson, the first of Niagara's great rivermen, piloted the steamer *Maid of the Mist* from her Canadian landing below the falls to Queenston, Ontario. The small vessel had proved unprofitable plying the tourist trade below the falls, so the owner sold her. The terms of the sale included the requirement to deliver the steamer to her new owner in the placid waters beyond the escarpment.

The *Maid of the Mist* had been built in the gorge to avoid the cost of lowering her to the waters she would navigate. In the end, the expense of hoisting her out of the gorge proved too much for the owner to bear. The only practical way to get her to Queenston was to send her through the Whirlpool Rapids.

Robinson's ride through the rapids.

In the afternoon of June 6, 1861, Joel Robinson steered the *Maid of the Mist* toward the head of the Whirlpool Rapids. His crew consisted only of an engineer named Jones and a machinist named MacIntyre. Hundreds of spectators watched from the gorge walls, fully expecting to witness the deaths of three fools.

At about 3:00 p.m., the tiny vessel passed beneath John Roebling's suspension bridge and lurched into the rapids under a full head of steam. With Robinson at the wheel, the *Maid* bounded through the raging waters unscathed until a wall of green water swept across the deck and leveled her smokestack. Somehow, Robinson kept her on course while his companions stoked the engine. A few minutes later, they were safe in the relatively calm waters of the Whirlpool.

When Robinson, Jones, and MacIntyre stepped ashore in Queenston, they walked into history as the first men to conquer the Whirlpool Rapids. Until their brief, tumultuous journey, the rapids had been considered unnavigable. Still, their success did not immediately inspire imitation. Nearly a quarter century passed before anyone again intentionally made the trip.

Throughout the latter decades of the nineteenth century the lower Niagara was the scene of an abundance of accidental deaths, suicides, and not a few mysteries. The *Niagara Falls Gazette* published this item in its July 28, 1897 edition:

FROM THE DEAD

Bottle With a Message in it Found Near
the Whirlpool

A water-soaked wooden bottle with a top screwed down tightly was found on the shore at the Whirlpool yesterday afternoon. Inside the wooden case was found a glass bottle around which was wrapped a scrap of paper. On the paper was penciled, apparently in a woman's hand, the following:

"Good-bye, I am gone. F. W. E."
"Buffalo, N. Y., June 20, 1897"

The identity of F. W. E. was never ascertained. The note was typical of Niagara suicides, and was accepted as evidence of yet another death.

The Whirlpool is a unique geological formation three miles below the falls. Here, in a rough bowl one thousand feet across, the river sweeps counterclockwise beneath itself in a great arc, changing the course of its flow from north-northwest to east-northeast. The gorge walls tower two hundred fifty feet over the surface of the Whirlpool, and the riverbed lies nearly two hundred feet deep beneath it.

Stories of grim discoveries at the Whirlpool have appeared on the front pages of local newspapers since at least the 1840s. This descriptive account appeared on page one of the *Daily Cataract Journal* on July 9, 1901:

ANOTHER BODY FOUND IN THE WHIRLPOOL
Badly Decomposed Remains of a Man Taken
From the Waters of the Lower
Niagara Yesterday Afternoon

Two small boys living at Niagara Falls, Ont., whose names are Walker and Ryan, wandered down the river yesterday. After amusing themselves for some time among the trees and shrubbery they sat down on the bank to gaze at the awful maelstrom of water in the Whirlpool. Soon they observed a dark floating object tossed about by the swiftly moving currents. On closer inspection the lads were convinced that it was the body of a man. Both hurried back to the village and informed Undertaker A. Butler of Queen Street. He notified Coroner Emes and Chief of Police Mains.

In the meantime, before the coroner had arrived on the scene, Harry Preston, the well known "King of the Whirlpool," had heard of the discovery and lost no time in going down. He rowed out in a small boat as far as safety would permit and awaited a good opportunity to hook the corpse. In this he was successful, and when the coroner, the undertaker and a policeman arrived at the Whirlpool Preston was standing guard over the body below.

On instructions given by Coroner Emes it was taken to the top of the bank and removed to Undertaker Butler's establishment.

The body is apparently that of a young man about 25 or 20 years of age, five feet nine inches tall and weighing about 160 pounds. It has the appearance of having been in the water for some time. The top of the head is gone but enough of the scalp remains to show that the man had a heavy head of black hair. The only clothing on the body was a pair of shoes and socks, one leg of the trousers, and a collar and tie. The shoe was a new square-toed style, about seven or seven and a half in size. The collar was No. 15½, and was marked "Rex Brand, high top." The tie was a bow, blue in color, with white polka dots. The teeth are in good shape, the upper front teeth being filled with gold.

When a Cataract Journal reporter visited Niagara Falls, Ont., at about 10 o'clock this morning Undertaker Butler was starting for Fairview Cemetery with the body, where he intended to inter it temporarily. He told the newspaperman that the decomposed condition of the remains would not admit of their being kept for a longer time. It is his opinion that the body passed over the falls, but nothing has so far developed that would give the slightest clue to identification. This is probably another of Niagara's countless mysteries.

Most victims of the falls and rapids eventually surface in the Whirlpool, though not everyone who ends up there is dead. Sixteen-year-old Edward Denny of Niagara

Falls, New York, while swimming with friends near the American Fall on June 18, 1921, found himself trapped in swift currents in the middle of the river. He was too far from shore to reach safety before drifting into the Whirlpool Rapids, so he swam to a log floating nearby and held on fast. Miraculously, Denny kept his grip on the log as it barreled through the white water. A few minutes later he entered the Whirlpool where he was later rescued. He became one of only a handful of individuals to survive an unplanned trip through the Whirlpool Rapids.

The Spanish Aero Car made its inaugural trip in 1916.

Most of the dead and living who enter the Whirlpool do so from upriver, but Mrs. Ruth L. Hyde of Bradford, Pennsylvania, arrived there by an unusual and spectacular route. The beautiful 30-year-old wife of wealthy oilman William P. Hyde came to Niagara Falls on August 11, 1934. The following day she hired a cab driver named William Groom to take her to the popular viewing spots about the falls and gorge.

She visited Prospect Point and Goat Island, Table Rock, and Luna Island—all of the places favored by Niagara suicides. Groom also took her to the Canadian side of the Whirlpool and accompanied her on the Spanish Aero Car, a scenic cable car attraction that to this day conveys tourists from one side of the Whirlpool to the other and back again.

When the Aero Car reached the center of the Whirlpool, Mrs. Hyde looked down at the water and said, "This would be a great place for a suicide."

Groom did not take her comment seriously. That evening he dropped her off at his taxi stand. Groom recalled later that before she walked away she told him, "This river has an awful fascination for me."

In the afternoon of August 13, Mrs. Hyde returned to the Whirlpool and purchased a ticket for a ride on the Spanish Aero Car. At about 3:45 p.m. she handed her purse to the operator, Harold Brooker Jr., and boarded the car with twenty-five other passengers.

Arthur J. McKinley and his 6-year-old daughter, Catherine, sat next to Mrs. Hyde on the trip. McKinley scarcely noticed her until Catherine pointed out that she was smoking a cigarette in brief, rapid puffs. As they neared the middle of the Whirlpool, McKinley watched the woman pitch her cigarette into the gorge. Suddenly she stood.

"Still I paid little attention," McKinley said later, "for I thought she was going to see the view from the other side, but she climbed onto the seat and leaped over the safety gate and dived as gracefully as a good diver into the water."

McKinley saw and heard her body strike the river more than two hundred feet below. Catherine McKinley and Harold Brooker Jr. also saw Mrs. Hyde's leap, though none of the other Aero Car passengers witnessed the tragedy.

Mrs. Hyde was later identified by documents found in her purse. Her family, including her 87-year-old husband, professed shock and grief, but could offer no motive for the suicide.

In June of 1972, a company billing itself as Niagara River White Water Tours conducted tourists through the gorge on huge rafts that carried twenty passengers and a crew of two. In two months of operation, at least thirteen passengers were dumped into the raging waters of the Whirlpool Rapids. All were rescued, but the warning signs were unmistakable: it would be but a matter of time before someone died. Niagara River White Water Tours ceased operations in August 1972.

In 1975, Toronto entrepreneur George Butterfield resurrected commercial rafting on the lower Niagara. In mid-August of that year, Butterfield's firm, Niagara River Gorge Trips, Inc., began test runs of the *Grider*, a $20,000 inflatable raft. The *Grider*, powered by a 40 horsepower outboard motor, was thirty-seven feet long and twenty-seven feet wide. Outrigger pontoons bound to the raft with cables buoyed the vessel.

The first ten trial runs of the *Grider* carried as many as thirty people, including volunteer passengers and crew. These trial runs were thrilling and apparently safe. George Butterfield was looking forward to charging tourists $20 apiece for the experience. The future of raft operations in the gorge looked bright and profitable until the midpoint of the eleventh trial run.

At 11:30 a.m. on August 29, 1975, the *Grider* picked up twenty-seven passengers at the American Maid of the Mist landing and headed downriver. As they motored toward the Whirlpool Rapids, the raft's two crewmen, Jerry Morton and Richard Overgaard, told the passengers how to sit, how to hold on to the safety ropes, and what to do if they were thrown into the water. They inspected life jackets to make sure they were worn properly by all aboard.

Twenty-two-year-old Marta DeSorcy was on the raft that day despite her fear of deep water. Her employer, George Butterfield, had invited her. She accepted the invitation because she thought it was safe. "Everything was fine and fun at first," DeSorcy said later. "Then we hit the first rapids—the big ones—and all of a sudden the front end just went straight up and there were people flying over my head."

Another passenger, *Courier Express* correspondent Dave Kewley, had a somewhat different recollection. "We got about midway," he said afterward, "when we hit a tremendous wave and there was a deep trough below us that might have swallowed the whole raft right then and there. The nose of the 37-foot raft lifted straight up in the air and flipped us over upside down when we hit the trough."

The *Grider* had encountered a "leaper," one of the huge waves that periodically surges up from the bed of the rapids. The leaper that capsized the *Grider* was twenty to twenty-five feet high. The great wave snapped one of the raft's pontoon cables and folded the vessel in half. DeSorcy, Kewley, and most of the other passengers ended up beneath the raft, clinging to ropes that served as handholds.

"Everybody had been yelling, but suddenly everyone was quiet," 21-year-old Richard Meech said afterward. "The next thing I knew I was in the water under the boat. I got out from under and saw a lot of heads bobbing around."

Kewley was one of the first to reach shore. He and two other men began pulling survivors from the water. They tried to resuscitate a woman who had been trapped under one of the raft pontoons. "She never showed any signs of recovery," Kewley recalled. "If I ever saw anyone who was dead, it was her."

New York State Park Police arrived at the scene in two tourist helicopters less than fifteen minutes after the *Grider* capsized. As police officers dragged people from the water, the helicopters plucked survivors from the river. Frank Edwards, the manager of Niagara Helicopter Tours, rode a sling beneath one of his helicopters during the rescue effort. As Edwards was making a grab for one of the people in the water, a wave swept him out of his sling. He ended up treading water in the Whirlpool until being rescued by his own aircraft.

The raft hugs the Canadian shore as it enters the Whirlpool Rapids on August 29, 1975.

By 4:00 p.m., all of the survivors had been ferried out of the gorge by helicopter. Twenty passengers had been injured or suffered hypothermia. Four required hospitalization. Three passengers drowned.

George Butterfield, who with his wife had watched the disaster unfold from a vantage point on the gorge rim, conducted a press conference later that day. "I'm still in a state of shock," he told reporters. "For two weeks things went so well. We were happy with the results and had some assurance. I'm very conscious of the people who died."

Immediately after the press conference Butterfield traveled by police cruiser to a morgue to identify the victims. Two of the dead turned out to be friends he had invited on the ill-fated trip.

The battered *Grider* came to rest on the Canadian shore along the southwest edge of the Whirlpool. On September 4, 1975, a jet boat piloted by Park Police mechanic Edwin G. "Bud" Schroeder Jr. sped upriver from Lewiston toward the Whirlpool to attempt a recovery of the raft. Accompanying him were Patrolmen James MacNeil and Richard Sutliffe of the Park Police.

There was no shortage of gawkers when the death raft finally berthed in the lower river.

The jet boat had been trucked down from the lesser rapids above the falls where it was employed for rescue operations. It proved unmanageable in the Devil's Hole Rapids, however. As Schroeder neared the mouth of the Whirlpool, white-capped

81

waves nearly swamped the boat. He struggled for a few minutes against the current, then brought the vessel about and headed back for Lewiston. When the boat was safely in calm waters, Schroeder suddenly slumped over the wheel and lost consciousness. Sutliffe and MacNeil radioed for an ambulance and tried to revive Schroeder with mouth-to-mouth resuscitation. Schroeder was pronounced dead on arrival at Mt. St. Mary's Hospital. He had suffered a heart attack.

Fifty-one-year-old Bud Schroeder was an experienced riverman and boat racer. A veteran of the U.S. Navy during World War II, he had survived three ship sinkings in that conflict. Schroeder was the final casualty of the *Grider* tragedy.

Although rafting has been banned in the lower rapids and Whirlpool for nearly a quarter of a century, accidents and suicides here have continued unabated. Yet, not all of the dead found in these waters arrived willingly or through mishap.

At 3:00 p.m. on July 23, 1995, New York Park Police recovered a body from the Whirlpool and handed it over to the care of Niagara County Coroner James Joyce. The dead man appeared to be about thirty years old. He was five feet ten inches tall and weighed 175 pounds. His hair was brown. His clothing contained no identification papers, but his body was distinctively tattooed.

The dead man proved to be 22-year-old Bobby Thompson, a Niagara Falls, New York, resident who had been missing since July 19. Joyce and the Park Police suspected foul play because Thompson's body revealed signs of blunt trauma, including severe head wounds. He had apparently been beaten before entering the water. An autopsy established the cause of death as drowning.

On Christmas Day, 1995, Niagara Falls Police received a telephone call from an informant who stated that Thompson had been murdered by three young men: Matthew J, Rolfe, his cousin Kerwin N. Rolfe, both of Lewiston, and William J. Clark of Niagara Falls, New York. When interrogated by Inspector Edward Stefik of the Niagara County Sheriff's Department, the trio admitted to the killing.

The Rolfes and Clark had beaten Thompson after an argument on July 19, 1995, then had thrown the helpless man into the river at the head of the Whirlpool Rapids.

On November 28, 1995, 24-year-old Matthew Rolfe was sentenced to fifteen years to life in a state prison for second-degree murder. Kerwin Rolfe and William Clark pleaded guilty to lesser charges.

8

ICE

At certain revolutions all the damned
Are brought; and feel by turns the bitter change
Of fierce extremes, extremes by change more fierce,
From beds of raging fire to starve in ice
Their soft ethereal warmth, and there to pine
Immovable, infixed, and frozen round . . .

—John Milton

Ice at Niagara has often caused spectacular property damage or death. It has also created some of the most breathtaking scenery to be found anywhere on the globe. Freezing mist produces beautiful warped trees and choirs of titanic icicles. On crisp January days, the American Fall becomes an ice palace. Crystalline mountains form on the talus below it, and falling water solidifies into gnarled columns that seem the fancy of a mad architect. In the bitter depths of winter, sunshine transforms Niagara into a glistening wonderland.

During most winters ice bridges form between the falls and the Whirlpool Rapids. During mid-winter thaws, the ice sheets on Lake Erie and the upper Niagara break up and move downstream. When these thaws are followed by periods of persistent high winds from the south and extreme low temperatures, continuous flows of pack ice crash over the falls and form jams in the gorge where the river is no more than one thousand feet wide. Sometimes the ice partially dams the lower river, collecting more ice until a natural bridge of crystallized water spans the gorge between Ontario and New York. Some ice bridges are not much broader than their man-made cousins, while others cover hundreds of yards of the river's length. The thickness of the ice ranges from thirty to more than one hundred feet.

For nearly a century the formation of an ice bridge was cause for celebration. Rivermen would erect shacks on the ice from which to sell souvenirs and liquor to sightseers. In those days before safety replaced amusement as a priority in North American pastimes, there was never a shortage of customers. Scores of thousands came to Niagara to explore the weird terrain of the bridges or to sled down the ice mountains below the American Fall.

Tourists on the ice bridge and ice "mountains," circa 1900. At left is the Inclined Railway.

But the ice bridges have always been dangerous. Calamity lurks in their crevasses and death waits patiently in the roiling pools that pock their frozen surfaces. Temperature increases and the immense stress the river exerts on the bridges eventually cause them to fracture—sometimes unexpectedly. When this happens they disintegrate into beds of slush and blocks of ice. The river then carries this debris into the Whirlpool Rapids, where the violent currents toss the massive blocks about like boulders in an avalanche.

In the blustery afternoon of February 28, 1886, a young wholesale liquor salesman named L. George DeWitt paid his first visit to Niagara Falls. He arrived on the 1:15

p.m. Michigan Central train from Buffalo. Eager to see the falls and the ice bridge in the gorge, DeWitt wasted no time in hiring a cab to carry him to the Inclined Railway at Prospect Park. He asked Jack McCloy, the Railway's wheelman, how long it would take to get to the bottom of the gorge. McCloy assured him the trip would last only a minute or two. DeWitt bought a ticket and began his descent a moment later.

Once in the gorge, DeWitt rented a rubber cap and a set of strap-on shoe spikes from guide John Conroy, brother of the famous riverman Thomas Conroy. As he changed his clothing, DeWitt mentioned that he was from New York City, and complained about the high cost of sightseeing at Niagara, but he did not give his name. He left his silk hat and two newspapers in Conroy's care before trudging out onto the ice.

DeWitt headed for the ice mountain that had formed on the talus below the falls. Rather than climb the mountain by means of the slope that merged with the ice bridge, he ascended along a path that took him between the vertical face of the mountain and the American Fall. He climbed to a ledge and stepped over a small fissure onto a flat section of ice that stretched out before the face of the fall. The ice seemed a solid platform from which to view the torrent of falling water, but it was not. The spray from the fall had eroded the ice beneath DeWitt's feet. He was actually standing on a thin shelf that could scarcely support its own weight. As he approached the edge to get a better view of the fall, the shelf collapsed.

DeWitt plummeted forty feet into a heap of ice shards and slush. He lay motionless for a moment, then slowly climbed to his feet. He was apparently uninjured, but as he stood in the midst of a whirlwind of spray from the fall, he stumbled backward into a fissure and vanished. An instant later, the rest of the shelf came crashing down behind him.

Sightseers on the ice mountain and along the gorge rim witnessed the accident and reported it to Jack McCloy and John Conroy. The wheelman and the guide rushed to the wall at Prospect Point to look for the missing man, but there was no sign of him. They quickly gathered coils of rope and a rope ladder then rode the Railway into the gorge. A handful of men at Prospect Point kept watch on the ice below.

McCloy and Conroy climbed to the summit of the ice mountain and attempted to lower the rope ladder, but the wind and whirling spray from the fall flung it about like a whip and coated the rungs with ice. Rescue by this route proved impossible, so they surveyed the path along the face of the mountain. The spot at which the man had fallen was inaccessible by this route, as well. They could only hope that the weather improved quickly so they could search for him.

By the end of the day, McCloy, Conroy, and the Reservation Police had given up all hope of finding the man alive. They were convinced that the second ice fall had killed him outright or had hurled him down through the fissure into the flood of water rushing beneath the mountain. Once they gave him up for dead, all that remained was to discover who he was and to notify his next of kin.

McCloy described the man to Reservation Police. He was thirty or thirty-five years old, five feet six inches tall, with sandy hair, sideburns and a mustache. He wore a dark suit, a brown overcoat, and the silk hat he had left with Conroy.

An examination of the hat revealed little. It bore the label of a New York City manufacturer. The inside band held a ticket folder from a Detroit travel agency dated February 26, 1886. The newspapers, recent editions of the *Buffalo Sunday News* and the *New York Tribune*, offered no clues.

As investigators received reports of missing persons they quickly narrowed the probable identity of the victim down to two men: L. George DeWitt and a traveling drug salesman named J. S. Marvin. Marvin had left his Buffalo hotel, the Tifft House, on February 28 and had not yet returned. On March 1, amid speculation that the man on the ice mountain had committed suicide, Marvin reappeared at his hotel. He had been visiting with friends in nearby Lancaster. When he learned that he was thought by some to be dead, he remarked, "I am the liveliest kind of suicide you ever saw in your life."

William Hurst, the desk clerk at the Broezel House in Buffalo, came to Niagara Falls on March 1 to speak with Reservation Police. Hurst suspected the missing man was L. George DeWitt, a Broezel House guest who had left his room just after noon on the previous day. Before leaving, DeWitt told Hurst that he was going to Niagara Falls. He never returned. When Hurst heard Jack McCloy's description of the missing man and saw the silk hat, he was convinced that it was DeWitt.

Documents found in DeWitt's room enabled police to locate his employer and family. The police shipped his personal effects to his relatives in New York City. No one expected to see L. George DeWitt again, alive or dead. The tragedy was soon almost completely forgotten.

On Thursday, March 11, 1886, the face of the ice mountain collapsed. Much to the surprise and dismay of Reservation Superintendent Thomas V. Welch, there on a newly exposed ledge lay the lifeless form of L. George DeWitt. The next morning Welch organized a ten-man body recovery team headed by Jack McCloy and John Conroy.

The team considered scaling down the face of the ice mountain by rope ladder, but Welch forbade that approach as too dangerous. He decided the safest approach was to remove part of the mountain with dynamite. By midday, blasting was underway on the slope of the ice mountain, but the explosive charges proved ineffective. The team abandoned the blasting at Welch's direction. The next morning the men began work on a tunnel that would run from the slope of the mountain to the ledge where the dead man lay. For four days they attacked the ice with axes, picks, and shovels.

As the work progressed, crowds of gawkers gathered at Prospect Point to view the corpse. The *Niagara Falls Gazette* observed:

> Ever since the announcement that the body could be seen from the top of the bank, the parapet wall has been lined, and for hours men and women would stand under a very heavy fall of spray, gazing over at the mangled remains of the unfortunate, each thinking themselves particularly favored if the spray would lift so that they could plainly see the mangled head. All day Sunday the Park was filled with this class of people.

When the tunnel was completed on Tuesday morning, March 16, it was more than sixty feet long, a little over five high, and nearly as wide. It ended in a vertical shaft that dropped twenty feet through the ice to a point near the body. Before noon, McCloy and Conroy climbed down the shaft on a rope ladder and broke through a wall of ice some four feet thick. They reached out into a gale of freezing spray and hauled the body from the ledge.

Documents found in the dead man's pockets confirmed that he was, indeed, L. George DeWitt. A coroner's jury determined that his death had been accidental. The top of his head had been "crushed off" by falling ice—or so the coroner's report stated.

Years later, John Conroy would claim that DeWitt had been trapped alive beneath the ice for days. Rather than face an agonizing death by exposure or starvation, he blew the top of his head off with a revolver. Conroy offered as evidence of his contention a handgun he found on the ice later that spring.

The DeWitt tragedy did nothing to deter tourists or locals from walking the ice bridges or climbing the ice mountains in 1886 or the ensuing decades. Even after January 22, 1899, the day upon which nearly one hundred sightseers barely escaped an ice bridge that broke up beneath their feet, people still flocked to the ice.

On February 1, 1904, this item appeared in the *New York Times*:

DOUBLE ESCAPE AT NIAGARA
Himself in Peril on a Detached Ice Floe,
a Man Rescues a Boy and Both
Are Saved.

NIAGARA FALLS, Jan. 31.—This afternoon, while hundreds were on the ice bridge below the falls, a large cake broke away from the bridge near the ice mountain. On it was John Morrison of this city. While the crowds were staring in fear at the man's predicament, there came a cry from the ice mountain, and a lad, James Murty, slid down into the open water left by the detached floe.

Morrison, in danger himself on the detached cake, which at any moment might have been swept down the gorge to the Whirlpool, saw the boy's danger. Lying flat on the floating ice he awaited the reappearance of the boy. As the lad came gasping to the surface of the ice-cold water, Morrison grabbed him by the hair and hauled him on the floe.

The crowds cheered Morrison to the echo, and soon ropes were got and cast to him. The floating ice was then slowly drawn to the bridge, and both Morrison and Murty leaped to safety.

The narrow escape of Morrison and Murty should have served as a warning to the police authorities on both sides of the river, but it did not. No real effort was made to keep the public off the ice below the falls until 1912.

The Upper Steel Arch Bridge before the great ice jam of 1938.

The wreckage of the Upper Steel Arch Bridge lay on the ice for months.

Ice in the gorge has frequently threatened human life and has sometimes claimed it, but its most memorable effects have been upon man-made structures. The great ice bridge of 1899 reared eighty feet above the river's surface, threatening to undermine the abutments of the new Upper Steel Arch Bridge, but work crews kept the ice at bay with dynamite. When the ice subsided, the bridge was still standing, and had suffered only minor damage.

In 1938 the great span did not fare so well. On January 25 of that year, one of the greatest ice jams in the history of the Niagara River swept down from Lake Erie and began to pile up in the gorge below the falls. The ice dammed the lower river sufficiently to raise the water level below the falls to fifty-nine feet above normal. Ice and water smashed through the windows of the hydroelectric plant of the Ontario Power Company, disabling the generators there. Ice filled the Cave of the Winds elevator shafts at the foot of Goat Island, and destroyed the Maid of the Mist dock facilities.

As ice continued to come over the falls, mountains of the stuff rose in the gorge. It soon began to pile up against the masonry abutments of the Upper Steel Arch Bridge. By 9:15 a.m. on January 26, ice had risen thirty feet above the abutments and pressed against the steel structure of the bridge itself. Girders and trusses began to bend as though made of rubber. American and Canadian authorities closed the bridge to traffic for the first time in its forty year history.

Shortly after 1:00 p.m., rivets began to shoot like bullets from the steel beams and cross members. Two large girders fell from the bridge. Later that afternoon the bridge decking developed a visible bulge. Work crews battled to clear the ice in a vain effort to save the bridge.

At 4:10 p.m. on January 27, 1938, the eight hundred forty-foot span of the Upper Steel Arch Bridge toppled into the Niagara Gorge. The massive steel structure lay shattered on the ice until mid-April, when it finally sank.

Most of the calamity caused by ice at Niagara has occurred in the lower river, but ice above the falls has produced its share of adventure and tragedy. On March 6, 1894, an unidentified woman went over the American Fall on an ice floe. No one knew how she came to be there, but three men, including Edwin Whitney, grandson of renowned hotelier Parkhurst Whitney, witnessed her fatal passage.

The United Press issued this wire story in March 1916:

FIVE CHINAMEN DROWNED IN THE NIAGARA RIVER
Embarked at Chippawa and
Were Caught in the Running Ice

Buffalo, N. Y., March 18 — Five Chinese were drowned in the Niagara River early in February when the rowboat in which they were smuggled from Canada to the United States caught in an ice jam near Navy Island and capsized. The smugglers saved themselves but failed to report the tragedy, fearing prosecution.

Chief of Chinese Inspectors Richard H. Taylor of New York made the above statement this afternoon., following an investigation covering two weeks. He said the Chinese embarked at Chippawa, Ont.

In the morning of February 4, 1930, 24-year-old Harry Bartley's motorboat began taking on water through a breach in the hull after colliding with an ice floe on the upper Niagara near Navy Island. Bartley tore off his coat and stuffed it into the opening, but the boat quickly filled with water. Shortly before noon, Bartley splashed into the river and climbed onto a passing sheet of ice. "I had a hard time clinging to the ice," he later told police, "because the water was so cold that my hands became numb, but I managed to crawl up on the floe and stick fast. My shoes froze to the ice, holding me on."

H. J. Campaigne, the marine engineer of the Niagara Falls Power Company, saw Bartley abandon the sinking boat. A few minutes later Campaigne and the crew of a company tug hauled Bartley from the ice a mile above the Canadian Rapids. Bartley's boat went over the Horseshoe Fall later that afternoon.

When asked by Niagara Falls Police what he had been doing on the ice-choked river, Bartley claimed to have been taking the boat on a test run. Prohibition was still in force, so it would have been natural for the police to guess that he had, in fact, been attempting to smuggle liquor, but Bartley stuck to his story.

"It was a close call for me," Bartley said from his hospital bed the next day. "I knew I was not far above the falls and I had about given up hope when they got me off."

On February 3, 1977, New York State Park Police warned visitors to the Niagara Reservation of the treacherous footing there. Over the harsh winter thick layers of snow and frozen mist had accumulated in Prospect Park and on the adjoining islands. The snow was nine feet deep in places.

On the southern edge of Goat Island, the slope of Porter's Bluff was buried under deep, hard-packed snow coated with ice. From the crest of the bluff to the brink of the Horseshoe at Terrapin Point stretched a steep, glazed surface that would have served well as a toboggan run.

At 1:30 p.m., two young men from Niagara Falls, New York, were on Porter's

Bluff photographing the fantastic winter scenery that glistened under blue skies and brilliant sunshine. Twenty-four-year-old John Jordan was clutching his camera at the crest of the bluff when his feet slipped from beneath him. In an instant he was flat on the ice-encrusted snow, accelerating downhill toward the brink of the Horseshoe Fall. He tried to slow himself, but there was nothing to grab. The ice was too thick to punch his fists through even if he had the time to try.

Patrolman James MacNeil approaches Jordan's position. The cylindrical objects protruding from the snow are the tops of twelve-foot street lamps.

Jordan slid two hundred feet in just a few seconds. When he reached the riverbank there was nothing to grab there, either—the guardrails were buried under six feet of snow and ice. He plunged into the Canadian Rapids less than one hundred feet from the brink of the Horseshoe. The swift current immediately carried him toward the gorge.

"I knew what was happening," Jordan recalled afterward, "but my mind was a blank. My head had gone under a few times." Fortunately, he recovered his senses quickly enough to save himself. "I was able to plant my feet and grab the ice along the shore." Somehow he stood and pulled himself far enough out of the water to peer over the wall of snow and ice along the riverbank.

Twenty-one-year-old Jeff Dennis watched in horror as his friend shot down the icy slope and splashed into the rapids. "I figured he was a goner," Dennis said later. Dennis began to scream for help. John Pasquantino, another city resident, heard his cries and rushed to the bluff. When Pasquantino saw Jordan, he dashed to the complex of buildings at the Cave of the Winds. There he encountered caretaker Frank Kranciz, who alerted the Park Police at their nearby headquarters.

A few minutes later the crest of Porter's Bluff was swarming with police officers and Reservation maintenance workers. Patrolman James MacNeil slipped into a rescue harness attached to a three hundred-foot length of rope and began working his way down the slope toward Jordan. A team of twenty men that included Park Police Captain Joseph DeMarco and Mario Pirastru, Regional Administrator of the Niagara Frontier State Park and Recreation Commission, paid out the rope. When MacNeil was about ten feet away from Jordan he threw him a coil of rope and told him to hold on tight. Jordan said nothing, but wrapped the rope around himself. At MacNeil's signal the men on the bluff hauled it in.

Jordan returned to the crest of Porter's Bluff twenty-five minutes after he had entered the river. A waiting ambulance rushed him to Niagara Falls Memorial Medical Center, where he quickly recovered from exposure. The only permanent injury he suffered was the loss of his camera.

After Jordan's rescue, Park Police closed Prospect Point and Goat Island to the public.

9

THE CUP OF TANTALUS

The Immanent Will that stirs and urges everything

Prepared a sinister mate
For her—so gaily great—
A Shape of Ice . . .

—Thomas Hardy

Pack ice jammed the river from the American Fall to the Upper Steel Arch Bridge beginning in mid-January, 1912. By January 26, an ice bridge had formed that was one thousand feet long and sixty to eighty feet thick. It was one of the most substantial ice bridges in Niagara's history.

Not all of the ice coming from upriver reached the bridge. Some of it lodged among the rocks along the Canadian shore just below the Horseshoe. What began as a small accumulation of ice soon grew into a congealed mass that jutted thirty feet above the water. By February 3, it had grown into an ice field that covered nearly three acres of the river's surface.

Early the next day, the temperature hovered just above 0° Fahrenheit. Despite strong southwest winds pelting the gorge with freezing mist, thousands of tourists were on hand to take in the scenery and walk the ice. The turnstile count at the elevators on the American side of the gorge passed two thousand that day; a similar number made the descent by way of the stairs nearby. A large crowd was in attendance on the Canadian side, as well. Hundreds of people spent the morning on the ice bridge, but by 11:30 the crowds had wandered off to find shelter and lunch. Shortly before noon fewer than thirty people remained on the ice. Among these stragglers were 36-year-old Eldridge Stanton and his wife, Clara.

These faded newspaper images are the only known
photographs of Clara and Eldridge Stanton

The Stantons had visited Niagara Falls at least once each summer since their marriage in 1905. They always took a room at the Allen Hotel on the New York side of the river. Eldridge was the secretary and treasurer of O. B. Stanton and Wilson Company, Ltd., his brother's printing and stationery firm. He had worked in the family company for twenty years and was a respected figure in the Toronto business community. He was an Anglican and a Mason in St. John's Lodge. Clara was the 28-year-old daughter of Nelson Butcher, a Toronto stenographer.

On Friday, February 2, 1912, the Stantons made their first winter trip to Niagara. They checked into the Allen that evening for a two-night stay. On Saturday morning, they purchased toboggan suits for protection against the harsh weather and set out on a tour of the city and the State Reservation. They strolled arm-in-arm, laughing and talking like newlyweds. Their plan was to return to Toronto on the 5:00 p.m. train the following day.

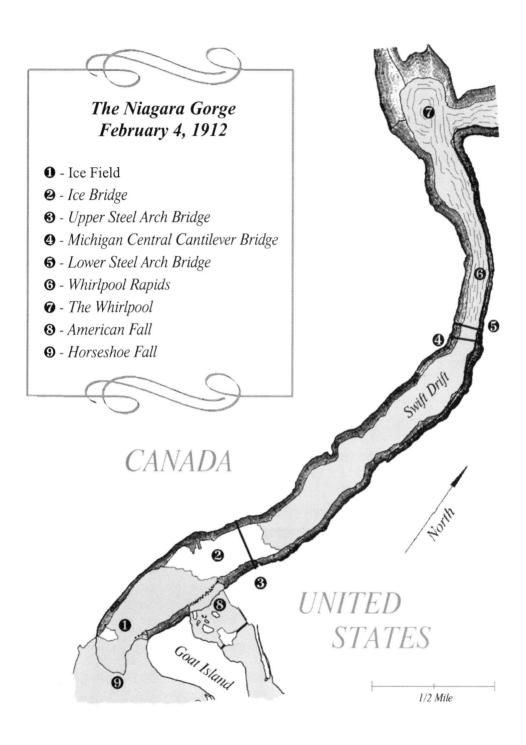

The Niagara Gorge
February 4, 1912

❶ - Ice Field
❷ - *Ice Bridge*
❸ - *Upper Steel Arch Bridge*
❹ - *Michigan Central Cantilever Bridge*
❺ - *Lower Steel Arch Bridge*
❻ - *Whirlpool Rapids*
❼ - *The Whirlpool*
❽ - *American Fall*
❾ - *Horseshoe Fall*

CANADA

UNITED
STATES

Swift Drift

North

Goat Island

1/2 Mile

On Sunday, February 4, the Stantons awoke at 9:00 a.m. and enjoyed a leisurely breakfast. At 10:30 they walked from the hotel to the State Reservation. They took an elevator into the Niagara Gorge and began to explore the fantastic landscape of the ice bridge. It was about 11:40 when they crossed the ice to the middle of the river a short distance above the Upper Steel Arch Bridge. There they exchanged pleasantries with Mr. T. A. Narraway and his friend, Edith Harris. Narraway and Harris said good-bye and headed for the American shore along a path that took them near the shack of riverman William "Red" Hill.

Hill had set up shop dispensing whiskey and trinkets to ice bridge tourists. He was looking forward to the afternoon crowds, as was his competitor, another riverman named William LeBlond. LeBlond had erected a shack on the ice not far from Hill's.

Near the shacks were several other sightseers: Michael Elmendorfer, a Lockport plumber, and his nephew, Philip Wending, a wrestler from Maple Grove, Michigan; Monroe Gilbert of Niagara Falls, New York; Ignatius Roth and Burrell Hecock, both of Cleveland.

Roth and Hecock were seventeen years old and had been friends since early childhood. Hecock worked as a purchasing clerk in the Lake Shore office of the Lehigh Valley Railroad. He took advantage of his position to travel by rail to Niagara Falls as often as he could. He was fascinated by the place and had visited the Falls many times. He and Roth had arrived by train from Cleveland on Saturday.

Late in the morning of February 4, Burrell Hecock was at his favorite place in the world with his best friend in the world. He was having the time of his life.

Just before noon the great ice field below the Horseshoe broke free of the rocks and headed downstream, probably as a result of pressure from the fierce wind and the great quantity of pack ice coming over the fall. It accelerated in the swift waters and was soon barreling along at about fifteen miles per hour.

James Coan and Harry Williams, both of Niagara Falls, Ontario, were looking into the gorge when the ice field began to move. With a handful of friends they initiated a general alarm, but their warning cries came too late.

At almost noon exactly, the ice field rammed the ice bridge with a sound like the cracking of a monstrous whip. The force of the impact and the added buoyancy of thousands of tons of ice and slush that shot beneath the bridge caused the massive span of frozen water to rise. As it moved upward, it pulled away from shore and began to fracture.

Only two people in the gorge immediately understood the significance of the loud noise and the movement of the ice beneath them: the rivermen. Hill and LeBlond had between them decades of experience watching the Niagara. They had seen many ice bridges come and go. They knew the signs. More importantly, they knew what lay downriver—the Whirlpool Rapids. Instantly they shouted out a warning to everyone on the bridge.

LeBlond ran to the security of the American shore.

Hill ran for Canada. "Follow me!" he cried to the nearest tourists. Monroe Gilbert and an Italian immigrant followed him and soon made it to safety.

Most of those on the ice saved themselves, but six confused sightseers remained in mid-river even as Hill scrambled ashore. By the time they decided to move, the ice bridge was disintegrating and accelerating toward the rapids. The air reverberated with the crashing sounds of breaking ice. The tremendous pressure exerted upon the bridge by the river was turning vast sections of the span into slush.

Hill ran back out on the bridge and implored the Stantons to escape to Canada, but they were paralyzed by indecision. Clara Stanton wanted to head for the American shore and Eldridge Stanton did not know what to do at all. Reluctantly, they followed Hill.

The riverman led them over ice mounds and through slush, from fragment to fragment of ice and across fissures in the failing bridge. The journey of two hundred yards seemed to take days. They were about fifty feet from the riverbank when Clara Stanton inexplicably dropped to her knees and refused to go further. Her husband then decided, equally inexplicably, to take her back toward the American side of the river. Hill argued with them, but they would not relent. In the end, he abandoned them and went ashore.

The Stantons turned about and retraced their steps, but as they neared the American shore a yawning chasm opened in their path. The weary couple could not jump across, so they reversed course and headed back toward Canada.

Burrell Hecock was taking pictures when the bridge came apart. When he realized what was happening, he dropped his box camera. Ignatius Roth retrieved it, but Hecock took it from him and threw it away. "This is no time to think of cameras," he said.

They were looking for a way off the ice when they saw the Stantons. Just then Clara Stanton stumbled and fell. Eldridge tried to pull her upright, but managed only to drag her.

"I can't go on!" she shouted. Then she moaned. "I can't go on. Let us die here."

Eldridge called out for help. Hecock went to his aid and helped pull the woman to her feet. As they hauled her along, Roth hurried on ahead toward Canada where Hill waited with a handful of firemen and Harry King, Superintendent of the Ontario Power Company. But the ice upon which the Stantons and the boys stood was breaking into fragments.

Michael Elmendorfer and Philip Wending heard Eldridge Stanton's call for assistance and hurried to lend a hand, but the ice began to break up around them, forcing them to turn back toward Canada. They scrambled over the crumbling bridge. In places they had to jump over fissures and wade through water that splashed up to their hips. By the time they reached shore they were completely exhausted and had to be pulled up the riverbank by Canadian firemen.

Roth was about one hundred twenty feet from the Upper Steel Arch Bridge when the ice beneath him broke away from the huge sheet carrying Hecock and the Stantons. He was now alone on a small floe awash with freezing water. He turned to look at Hecock. "Can't you make it?" he called out.

"No," was Hecock's grim reply. "Good-bye. Don't tell my mother."

Word of the looming catastrophe spread quickly in the cities overlooking the gorge. Customs officers on both ends of the Upper Steel Arch Bridge telephoned the fire and police departments. Within minutes hundreds of uniformed men converged on the gorge. Even a contingent of Canadian fire ladies joined the rescue effort.

Chief Newman of the Niagara Falls, Ontario, Fire Department rushed to the Upper Steel Arch Bridge and led a fire crew into the gorge. Newman and his men clambered over the ice-strewn riverbank to a point opposite Roth, Hecock, and the Stantons. They arrived just in time to help Elmendorfer and Wending to safety.

When Roth became separated from his companions, Red Hill went to his aid. He scrounged a length of rope from Newman's men and ran along the shore. The boy was several hundred feet out in the river, but there was a chance he could reach safety if he moved quickly and chose the right path. Hill shouted instructions as he ran. Several firemen joined him, calling out and gesturing to the boy.

Roth leaped from his ice floe to one adjacent. The men ashore indicated which cake of ice to move to next. With the ice about him grinding into slush and splinters as it passed beneath the Upper Steel Arch Bridge, Roth walked, ran, and hopped as he was told. A gaping water hole stopped his progress about seventy-five feet from safety, but he somehow got around the obstacle. When he was fifteen feet from shore Hill threw him the rope. The boy seized it and slogged through waist-deep water until he was near enough for Hill to drag him up the riverbank. Two hundred fifty yards below the Upper Steel Arch Bridge, Ignatius Roth was on solid earth and safe at last.

T. A. Narraway and Edith Harris made it unassisted to the American side shortly after Roth's escape from the ice.

Meanwhile, Newman's American counterpart, Chief Otto Utz, dispatched every available man from several fire houses. Utz and his men went to the Upper Steel Arch Bridge with an aerial truck. The big vehicle proved impossible to maneuver into any useful position, so the firemen raced to intercept the ice at the old Maid of the Mist landing above the Whirlpool Rapids.

As the ice moved inexorably downriver Hecock and the Stantons seemed to wander aimlessly. At length they dropped to their knees. The floe upon which they rested grew ever smaller as it collided with other fragments of the ice bridge.

The Michigan Central Railroad Cantilever Bridge and the Lower Steel Arch Bridge spanned the Niagara Gorge at the head of the Whirlpool Rapids.

Assistant Fire Chief Woods ordered every man of the Tenth Street Station down to a rock ledge on the American shore near the Michigan Central Railroad Cantilever Bridge and the Lower Steel Arch Bridge. Woods and his men waited there to throw rescue lines to Hecock and the Stantons, but their ice floe never came nearer than one hundred feet of shore. The firemen could only watch as the trio floated through Swift Drift, the last stretch of calm water before the rapids.

Fireman A. Scott still thought something could be done. If the people on the ice tried to swim for shore they might last long enough to reach for a thrown rope. "For God's sake," he shouted, "make an effort here! The rapids are ahead of you!"

Hecock got to his feet and gazed at Scott. He seemed to steel himself for a leap into the frigid green water.

Scott urged him on. "This is your last chance!"

But Hecock did not make the attempt. As the floe continued downriver he turned to rejoin the Stantons. Before he could reach them the ice fractured once again. Just before 1:00 p.m. a powerful eddy held the Stantons back while Burrell Hecock whirled through Swift Drift on his own great slab of ice.

Upper left: the Stantons huddle on a slab of ice trapped in an eddy while Burrell Hecock floats toward the bridges and the Whirlpool Rapids.

Above: the Stantons enter rough water.

Left: the shacks of Red Hill and William LeBlond move downstream along the Canadian shore. The structure in the background is the Upper Steel Arch Bridge.

For a moment the boy stood motionless with his hands in his pockets. Suddenly, he heard shouting from above and looked up at the fast-approaching cantilever bridge. There he saw the pale faces of men at the railing pointing wildly downward. Hecock lowered his gaze and saw a rope dangling from the bridge a short distance ahead. There was still hope. Burrell Hecock readied himself for a last chance at Salvation.

Men of a Michigan Central repair gang were at work on the cantilever bridge when word of the emergency reached them. Chuck Steelow, a riveter, sprinted along the ties to the American end of the bridge. He grabbed a huge coil of one-inch rope stored there and lugged it out onto the span. Alexander Croft, the gang foreman, along with John Venner and Thomas Beal, rushed to help him. Another group of railroad workers and Pat Kelly, a Canadian police officer, soon reinforced them.

The men on the bridge dragged the rope to a point at which they judged Hecock would pass, and dropped a two hundred foot length over the railing. Hecock was moving so quickly that there was not enough time to tie a loop or even a knot at the end of the rope. The railroad men could only pray that the boy on the ice below could grab the rope and hang on.

Hecock removed his coat and waved at the Stantons, then turned and readied himself. The ice floe bounded upward just as the rope came within reach. He took it in both hands as the ice settled back into a trough and slipped away beneath him. As the rope took his full weight, it stretched and dunked him up to his chest in the river.

As soon as Hecock grabbed the rope, more than twenty men began the mad work of hauling him to the deck of the cantilever bridge. As fast as the rescuers reacted, however, they could not keep him out of the water. In the moment it took them to pull Hecock from the river, three passing ice floes rammed into his body.

Frozen and battered, the boy somehow kept his grip on the rope. At first he tried to climb hand over hand, but he was too weak or too badly injured to continue. He held desperately to the lifeline and tried to wrap his legs around it, but as the men on the bridge pulled him further from the water the savage winds caused the rope to spin. Soon he was whirling dizzily thirty feet above the water.

It was about 1:10 p.m. when Croft and his companions hauled Hecock out of the river. They were determined that at least one of the ice bridge victims would be saved. Their hope for success increased with each foot of Hecock's ascent, but all hope evaporated when the boy was sixty feet above the river.

Hecock's hands began to slip—perhaps from fatigue, possibly because of ice on the hemp line. He tried to take the rope in his teeth, but couldn't; he was completely exhausted. His head fell back and he let go of the rope. For a sickening instant he hovered, flailing madly for a handhold. Then he fell.

He landed face-down on another floe. He stood and tottered briefly on ice brightly stained with his blood. Then the floe entered the rapids and capsized, pitching him into the river. For a few seconds he managed a pathetic breast stroke, but a wave engulfed him and he vanished.

The river had scarcely finished with Hecock when the eddy that had briefly spared the Stantons released them. They bobbed into the same current that had seized Hecock, and resumed their voyage. Eldridge had witnessed the boy's ordeal, yet he now stood calmly with Clara huddled at his feet. He watched as the men on the bridge lowered the rope once again.

The wind howled and the ice lurched underfoot as Eldridge removed his toboggan coat. He quickly helped Clara out of her coat, then he turned and waited. When the ice floe shot under the cantilever bridge, he seized the rope.

The men above paid out the line and Eldridge took up the slack. He attempted to tie the rope around his wife, but the river carried him to the end of the hemp line before he could complete the task. When it leapt from his hands he seemed at first dismayed, then once again hopeful: he saw another rope dangling a short distance downstream.

The men of the Niagara Avenue fire house on the American side were among the last to learn of the disaster. They arrived at the Lower Steel Arch Bridge, a stone's throw downstream from the cantilever, just in time to lower a rope in the Stanton's path. Like the men on the cantilever bridge they correctly judged that there was no time to prepare a noose or seat of any sort at the end of the line: as soon as their rope reached the water, Eldridge Stanton was there to grab it.

He caught it as before, and the men on the bridge gave him slack as the others had done. Again he tried to secure it about Clara's waist, but by this time his hands had frozen. He could not tie a knot. He fumbled for an agonizing moment then watched the end slip into the seething green waters.

Just before they entered the Whirlpool Rapids, the Stantons embraced and knelt on the ice as if in prayer. Miraculously, they passed unscathed through they first great wave. Then the second wave, a towering green wall, rolled over them. They were not seen again.

A close watch was kept on the Whirlpool and the lower river for weeks after the disaster, but the bodies of Eldridge Stanton, Clara Stanton, and Burrell Hecock never surfaced.

Ignatius Roth remained at Niagara Falls only long enough to answer questions put to him by newsmen and police officials. He returned home by the 5:00 p.m. train on February 4. His brother Walter, an undertaker, met him at the station in Cleveland.

Harry Hecock, Burrell's father, responded to a telegram informing him of the tragedy by taking the first available train to New York. His wife remained in Cleveland hoping against hope that her only child was still alive. When Harry Hecock learned the details of his son's death, he said, "Thank God. I can go back and tell her the lad died a hero."

A group of witnesses petitioned the Carnegie Hero Fund Commission to acknowledge Hecock's bravery. The Commission declined to honor the boy with the prestigious Carnegie Medal. The Commission retains records for only two years in cases in which no medal is awarded, so it is impossible to learn what considerations led to this decision.

Not long after the tragedy, a bronze tablet was placed in Queen Victoria Park on the Canadian side of the river. This humble monument was inscribed:

TO
THE MEMORY OF
BURRELL HECOCK
OF
CLEVELAND OHIO
AGED 17 YEARS
WHO LOST HIS LIFE IN AN
HEROIC ATTEMPT TO RESCUE
MR AND MRS
ELDRIDGE STANTON
OF TORONTO ONTARIO
WHEN THE ICE BRIDGE IN
THE GORGE IMMEDIATELY
BELOW WAS SWEPT DOWN
THE NIAGARA RIVER
AND INTO THE
WHIRLPOOL RAPIDS
FEBRUARY 4TH 1912

Red Hill contracted pneumonia as a result of exposure in rescuing Ignatius Roth. He recuperated and lived to become one of Niagara's most celebrated heroes.

William LeBlond, in his haste to escape the crumbling ice bridge, had abandoned the shack that held his supply of liquor and souvenirs, and his pet fox terrier. The sheet of ice carrying the shack came to rest along the American shore above the rapids. The terrier could be heard whining piteously throughout the afternoon and evening of February 4. Early the next day LeBlond rescued his dog and stock.

Witnesses to the tragedy reflected upon the horror of the day's events. There was plenty of blame, grief, and frustration to go around. The sense of futility and dismay that haunted many, but especially the would-be rescuers, was perhaps best expressed in this letter to the editor of the *New York Tribune*, published February 7, 1912:

> Sir: The press accounts of the horrible tragedy at Niagara Falls convey the impression that the ropes let down from the bridges had no loops at the ends. Such neglect is most incredible, and yet we read of the vain attempts to "tie" the ropes.
>
> Can the human mind conceive of the anguish of mind of those doomed people if they found only a bare end of rope presented to them? Loops in which to step or sit would mean safety; their absence, death. The cup of Tantalus would be a delight in comparison.
>
> J. H. N.
>
> New Milford, Conn.

Authorities on both sides of the river have prohibited tourists from walking on the ice bridges since February 4, 1912.

19

FAILURE

If a task is once begun
Never leave it till it's done.
Be the labor great or small,
Do it well or not at all.

—Unknown

Of the multitude of people who have come to Niagara Falls to kill themselves, few have failed. Some of those who fall short of the mark discover at the last instant that they are physical cowards unable to commit suicide at all. Others, initially attracted by the glamour of the place, find themselves intimidated by the water. Such was the case of Lucile Charter, who came from Ohio in 1901 to fling herself into Niagara's abyss. She could not bring herself to wade into the torrent or leap from a convenient bridge. Instead, she killed herself in a Niagara Falls, Ontario, hotel room with an overdose of morphine.

Some Niagara suicides reverse their opinion of self-destruction the moment they enter the cold water of the upper river. With luck, a police officer or a courageous tourist alters their course to oblivion, though luck is in short supply there.

Luck sometimes eludes rescuers, as well. There have been numerous rescues of would-be suicides at Niagara, but many attempts have failed miserably. Happily, no one has ever died trying to haul a suicide from the river, or talk one down from a bridge railing. Sadly, some persons who deserve a gruesome death at Niagara are rescued.

Reservation Patrolman Thomas Burch was making his rounds of Goat Island at sunset on September 12, 1892, when two tourists approached him and reported a young woman acting strangely on Luna Island. By the time he reached the tiny island it was almost completely dark. He had to feel his way around with his walking stick.

Burch saw no one and could hear nothing but the thundering roar of the falls. After searching for a few minutes, his stick encountered something lying on the ground near the brink of the American Fall. Upon closer inspection, the patrolman saw it was a bundle containing a pair of shoes, stockings, a straw hat, and a gold ring.

"She's gone," Burch said to himself, convinced that a young woman had gone over the fall. He began a search of the island's perimeter to be certain. Forcing his head and arms through the thick shrubbery lining the north shore, he looked down at the water's edge. There on a large rock no more than thirty feet from the brink of the fall sat a woman with her feet dangling in the rapids. As Burch stood considering how to proceed, she turned and looked up at him.

Even in the failing light, Burch could see that she was no more than sixteen years old. He could also see that she was pushing herself from the rock into the rapids. "Don't do that little girl!" he shouted as he scrambled through the bushes. "Wait a minute! I want to talk to you."

She held onto the rock, apparently interested in what he had to say.

Burch said anything he could think of to convince her not to kill herself. He begged her, pleaded with her, coaxed her.

When Burch stopped talking, she said, "I'm going to kill myself." Her words were punctuated with sobs. "My stepmother abuses me and I don't care for life."

Burch resumed his pleading, even as he crept close enough to grab her. "Here, give me your hand anyway," he said. But as he stretched his arm toward her, she turned toward the river and released her grip on the rock.

Burch sprang forward and grabbed the girl by one arm before the current carried her away. She struggled briefly, but he quickly dragged her ashore.

The girl turned out to be 15-year-old Ethel Lynman of Niagara Falls, New York. When Burch told her he would take her home, she said she would rather die than go back there. Her father, John Lynman, collected her from police headquarters later that night.

At 7:45 a.m. on September 23, 1898, two amateur photographers made a horrifying discovery in Prospect Park. While looking for a good vantage point from which to take pictures of the American Rapids, they found a corpse in the undergrowth along the riverbank near the Goat Island Bridge.

The dead man was 30-year-old George F. Franklin, a railroad brakeman from Rochester. Franklin had apparently come to the park the night before to throw himself into the rapids, but when faced with the prospect of going over the fall, his nerve failed. Instead, he spread a newspaper on the ground among the bushes, and lay down upon it. Then he pressed the muzzle of a .32 American Bulldog revolver to his head and pulled the trigger. Franklin left no note or other clue that would explain his suicide.

Shortly before 6:00 p.m. on April 3, 1902, a young woman named Delia Tansey leaped into the American Rapids from the Goat Island Bridge. The shock of the frigid water apparently produced a change of heart, for she began screaming for help and clawed at passing rocks to slow her progress to the American Fall.

A British tourist named William Connor was on Bath Island when he saw Tansey in the rapids. Without hesitation, he jumped in and waded out to intercept her, but she floated by just beyond his reach. Connor returned to the island and ran downstream to wade in for another attempt. This time he had better luck. Standing in waist-deep water about fifteen feet from shore, Connor grabbed Tansey's dress and held on tight.

By this time, she could do nothing to help save herself. Connor could do nothing to save her either—she was dead weight with the force of the river behind her. He screamed for help

Patrolman Thomas Burch heard Connor and ran to his assistance. Along the way he grabbed the nearest thing he could find that might be of use—a garden rake. He splashed into the river and wound Tansey's dress around the rake. Connor meanwhile transferred his grip from the dress to Tansey's foot, but her shoe slipped off. She floated away from him before he could reestablish his hold on her.

Burch maintained a firm grip on the rake, but the strain on the dress was too great. The material tore away from Tansey's body. She shot downstream and out into deep water. Moments later, she reached the brink of the American Fall, but she did not pass over. Her body became lodged in an ice jam at the lip of the precipice. A crowd gathered and stared helplessly at her motionless form until darkness hid her from sight. The following morning she was gone.

Afterward, Connor said, "If I could only have saved that woman's life, I would have been happy. Her cries as she drifted away to death will always ring in my ears."

Tansey left her pocketbook on the bridge. Its contents included $3.60, some keys, a handkerchief, and this note:

> Lived at Delaware Avenue for the past three years and I must say Miss Sill has driven me to do away with myself, as I would rather do that than lose the love of my own sister. Goodbye to all. I am going over the falls.

Miss Sill was the sister of Henry S. Sill of Buffalo, Delia Tansey's employer. Tansey worked in the Sill home as a domestic servant. She had apparently conducted a romantic affair with a married man, and had actually met with him on occasion at the Sill residence. When Henry Sill's sister learned of the affair, she told Tansey that the man could no longer come to the house, and cautioned her about seeing him at all. Delia Tansey heeded the warning and ended the affair at Niagara Falls.

In the afternoon of August 13, 1902, 60-year-old Adam Witzel of Buffalo waded into the rapids from Prospect Park about four hundred feet above the American Fall. The current swept him off his feet and carried him toward the gorge. Several tourists began shouting when Witzel entered the water. A group of men responded by rushing to Prospect Point to attempt a rescue.

Captain Frank Morse and Jacob Anthony, a Reservation patrolman, formed a human chain with two other men by holding hands. Morse waded out into the rapids a short distance from the fall while the other men planted their feet on the slimy riverbed and anchored him to shore.

Morse was lucky enough to intercept Witzel by grabbing his coat as he passed by. Witzel's momentum caused the human chain to swing toward the fall, however. Morse had a secure grip on the man's coat and had no intention of letting go. Inexplicably, the next man in the chain panicked and released his grip on Morse. Morse tried to hold Witzel in place, but could not. His feet began to skitter along the riverbed. Witzel was dragging him toward the fall. Morse had to let go of him to try to save himself. As Morse struggled ashore, Witzel dropped over the fall.

The man who had broken the chain was never identified. He fled the park as soon as he climbed out of the water.

Adam Witzel's battered corpse surfaced near the American Maid of the Mist docks on August 18.

In the morning of August 5, 1932, Park Police were scouring Prospect Point and Goat Island for any sign of a Rochester man who had reportedly come to Niagara Falls to kill himself. Oddly, two suicides were thwarted that day, though neither of them was the man from Rochester.

At 10:00 that morning, fifty-year-old John Tikehel of Detroit climbed the railing at Terrapin Point, but Park Police Officer Samuel Rhodes hauled him to safety. Rhodes lectured Tikehel then ordered him to leave. Tikehel walked up the path along the Canadian Rapids and began climbing the railing once again. Rhodes sprinted to Tikehel's side and handcuffed him before he could step into the water. Tikehel was arrested and charged with vagrancy.

Later that day, 33-year-old Clara Harris plunged into the rapids from the head of Goat Island. As she began to move toward the Horseshoe Fall, Jose Roberts saw her and ran to a storage box that contained a life line. Roberts handed one end of the rope to Howard Lochner, a tourist from Grand Rapids. Lochner held the rope while Roberts went into the river after Harris.

Roberts, a short, wiry man, had a difficult time with Harris, who weighed nearly two hundred pounds. Fortunately, she had not yet entered the deep, swift water, and Roberts was able to subdue her. With Lochner's help, Roberts got her safely back to

Goat Island, but he was completely exhausted. For his heroic effort, Roberts was later nominated for a Carnegie Medal.

The long list of failures at Niagara is not composed entirely of would-be suicides and luckless rescuers. Sometimes the failures are of sobriety or intelligence. Or both.

In the evening of July 6, 1951, Adolph Fuchs and his common law wife, Viola May Savery, both of Niagara Falls, Ontario, crossed the Whirlpool Rapids Bridge to the American side of the river. They visited with friends for several hours and consumed a fair amount of liquor. In the early morning of July 7, they headed for home.

At about 2:45 a.m., the reached the middle of the Whirlpool Rapids Bridge on the return trip. Savery, who was intoxicated, suddenly said to Fuchs, "I'm a better acrobat than you!" To prove it, she climbed to the top of the outside railing and began to walk as though on a tightrope.

Fuchs walked alongside her, supporting one of her outstretched hands to help her remain upright. She managed to walk for only a few feet before she lost her balance. William Howard, a Customs Officer at the Canadian end of the bridge saw her swaying as she placed one foot in front of the other on the railing. Finally, she swayed too far to the river side of the railing, and fell. Fuchs grabbed her by the hand and stopped her fall, but she was now dangling precariously two hundred feet above the head of the Whirlpool Rapids.

Assistance was already on the way when Fuchs began screaming for help. Howard began running as soon as he saw the woman fall. Murray Shannon, a toll collector, and Immigration Officer Vernon Pope joined him. Howard arrived just in time to make one attempt to grab Savery's arm, but at that moment Fuchs's grip failed. Savery plummeted into the darkness.

The Niagara Falls, Ontario, Fire Department deployed spotlights and fire crews to search the rocky shore of the gorge, but they could find no sign of Savery. The search was called off at 7:00 a.m. when they received word that the U. S. Coast Guard had recovered her body at the mouth of the river.

Violet May Savery was thirty-six years old.

Brenda Jeffs pulled into her driveway at about 9:20 a.m. on April 20, 1998, and saw a 26-year-old Jermaine Humphrey running toward her car. Humphrey lurched to her window and said, "I need help. I've been stabbed." He then slumped against her house. Jeffs dialed 911 on her cellular telephone to report the incident. An ambulance soon arrived and rushed him to Niagara Falls Memorial Medical Center, but he died of multiple stab wounds before anything could be done to save him.

The Niagara Falls, New York Police began their investigation into Humphrey' death at the home of Brenda Jeffs. They followed a blood trail from her driveway across the street to the residence of Joseph T. Spina, a 50-year-old maintenance worker employed by Occidental Chemical. Police officers entered the home and found a pool of blood, a bloody butcher knife, and signs of a violent struggle in the kitchen. They also found the lifeless body of Spina's third wife, Sara, in a blood-spattered bedroom on the second floor of the house.

Humphrey had been arrested several times on drug charges and was suspected by police of dealing crack cocaine. The police knew Joe Spina, as well. He had a record of drug arrests dating back to 1970. Police interviews with Spina's neighbors and friends suggested that he had been bingeing recently on crack cocaine. Some of his neighbors told police that he and his wife argued regularly about money. The were getting a divorce, police learned, though they continued to live in the same house. The previous day Spina told his neighbors that his wife was away visiting her sister.

Investigating officers speculated that Spina had killed his wife during an argument and then murdered Humphrey in a drug deal gone awry. The police began looking for Joe Spina later that day.

Spina had spent the night of April 19 at the home of his friend, Faith Carpenter. He left at 6:00 in the morning of April 20. Carpenter told police that Spina returned later that morning with a deep cut on his hand. He explained away the injury by saying that a drug dealer had attacked him. Carpenter also told police he had in his possession at least a thousand dollars worth of crack cocaine "rocks."

That afternoon, Spina asked Jamie Carlin, Carpenter's cousin, to accompany him in a taxi to Prospect Park. Carlin agreed. Once they were in the park, Spina said to her, "I've got to tell you something. Don't be nervous. Don't be scared. Do you think I'm a nice person?"

"Yes," Carlin answered.

As if to show Carlin that she could not be more wrong, Spina then said, "Me and my wife got into a fight two days ago and I killed her. A drug dealer came to my house today and I stabbed him four or five times in the chest and I beat him in the head with a hammer." He did not mention Humphrey by name.

"He said he was going to jump over the falls and kill himself," Carlin later told the police. "He said he'd rather do that than spend the rest of his life in jail."

Spina wanted Carlin to escort him down to the rapids above the American Fall, but she refused and fled.

City police were still looking for Spina when they received a report from State Park Police that Spina had been spotted pacing along the American Rapids between the Goat Island Bridge and Prospect Point.

Lieutenant James Lincoln, Detective Frank Granto, and Detective Carl Berak of the Niagara Falls Police Department went to the park immediately. State Park Police officers approached Spina, but he crawled down the riverbank to the edge of the rapids as if to wade in. He was still there, clinging to a tree branch, when the city police arrived.

Spina made it clear at the outset that he was going to enter the rapids and go over the fall. "It's either this," he told police, "or twenty-five years to life." He stepped into the water several times for emphasis.

Berak, Granto, and Lincoln pleaded with him to move away from the water. As they tried to talk him out of suicide, Spina wept and smoked crack cocaine from a small pipe.

"The entire time he was smoking crack—rock after rock," Lincoln later said. "He was extremely paranoid. He kept looking into the water like frogmen were going to jump out and get him."

Spina's paranoia was well-founded. There *were* frogmen in the water. Divers from the Park Police Swift Water Rescue Team and city firefighters waited downstream to attempt to intercept him if he left shore.

The city police asked two of Spina's coworkers at Occidental to try to convince him to surrender. They even called in a Roman Catholic priest, Monsignor William Stillwell of St. Mary of the Cataract Church.

The negotiations dragged on for more than two hours as Spina consumed rocks of crack and smoked cigarettes. The drama finally ended at 9:20 p.m., when Spina exhausted his supply of crack cocaine. He surrendered to police and was later charged with two counts of second degree murder.

Spina's trial began on September 11, 1998. The evidence against him was damning. The brutality of the crimes was incomprehensible. Jermaine Humphrey had been stabbed ten times and struck in the head with a hammer. Forty-three-year-old Sara Spina had been stabbed in the chest and neck. Blows to her head had fractured her skull.

The trial concluded on September 17, when the jury returned guilty verdicts on two counts of second degree murder after only two hours of deliberation.

On October 28, 1998, presiding Judge Charles J. Hannigan sentenced Joseph T. Spina to two consecutive terms of twenty-five years to life imprisonment. Spina's current residence is the Attica Correctional Facility. He will not be eligible for parole until April 15, 2048.

11

SWAN SONGS AND HORSEFEATHERS

And God blessed them, and God said unto them, Be fruitful, and multiply, and
replenish the earth, and subdue it: and have dominion over the fish of the sea,
and over the fowl of the air, and over every living thing that moveth upon the
earth.

—Genesis 1:28

Parkhurst Whitney, the youngest son of a prominent Massachusetts family and distant cousin of inventor Eli Whitney, took up residence on the New York side of the Niagara River in 1810. During the War of 1812 he held a Captain's commission under General Winfield Scott, and was captured by British forces at the Battle of Queenston Heights. In 1820, Whitney was promoted to Major General of the 24th Division, New York Militia. On the occasion of the opening of the Erie Canal in 1825, Whitney entertained as his personal guest the legendary Marquis de Lafayette.

When the war ended in 1814, Whitney leased the Eagle Hotel and established himself as a tireless promoter of Niagara Falls as a tourist resort. By 1838 he owned large tracts of land near the falls, including the renowned Cataract Hotel. Whitney built the first stairway into the gorge on the American side of the river, and helped organize the first ferry service below the falls. He was widely respected for his business acumen, generosity, and civic leadership. The Three Sisters Islands are named for his daughters Asenath, Angeline, and Celinda Eliza. Solon Island is named for his son. Despite his many noteworthy accomplishments, General Parkhurst Whitney is now largely forgotten. If he is remembered at all today, it is for his role in the *Michigan* affair.

In the summer of 1827, Canadian hoteliers William Forsyth of the Pavilion and John Brown of the Ontario House approached Whitney to devise a plan to lure tourists to the falls. The trio concocted a scheme that would today be the focal point of a criminal investigation and public outrage, but at the time was considered great entertainment.

Forsyth, Brown, and Whitney, together with a group of steamboat owners and stagecoach operators, purchased the *Michigan*, the largest schooner operating on Lake Erie at that time. The decrepit vessel had recently been declared unseaworthy, but the three Niagara hoteliers believed they could profit greatly from her final voyage. Their plan was simple: they would send the *Michigan* over the Horseshoe Fall. The spectacle of an unmanned ship plunging over the mighty cataract would no doubt draw spectators, but the prospect of death associated with the stunt would bring throngs of them. Forsyth, Brown, and Whitney intended to provide such a prospect by loading the ship with domestic and wild animals.

On August 2, 1827, Whitney produced a handbill announcing the event would take place on September 8, at 3:00 p.m.. The advertisement promised great efforts would be made to provide the *Michigan* with a crew of "Panthers, Wildcats, Bears, and Wolves" or at least "a few vicious or worthless Dogs" and "Lesser Animals." It circulated widely in the region and produced the desired effect. Several days before the event, stagecoaches, boats from the Erie Canal, and carriages converged on Niagara Falls. On September 7, wagons bearing farmers and their families began pouring into the vicinity. The hotels belonging to Forsyth, Brown, and Whitney filled to capacity in no time. Their kitchens and bars had more customers than they could handle.

On Saturday morning, September 8, five of the six steamboats operating on Lake Erie came down the river from Buffalo and Black Rock. The *Niagara*, *William Penn*, *Pioneer*, and *Henry Clay* were crowded with passengers, as was the *Chippawa*, the vessel assigned to tow the *Michigan* into position above the Canadian Rapids. Each steamboat carried a band that played rousing tunes as the flotilla chugged down the broad blue river under a blazing sun.

The *Chippawa* towed the *Michigan* to a temporary anchorage three miles above the Horseshoe and deposited her passengers on the Canadian shore. The other vessels unloaded their human cargo on both sides of the river. Immediately, caravans of wagons, stagecoaches, carriages, and mounted men headed for the falls.

When the *Michigan* weighed anchor at 3:00 p.m., as many as thirty thousand people waited in breathless anticipation along the banks of the river. A yawl with a crew of five oarsmen led by Captain James Rough towed the *Michigan* to within a quarter mile of the Canadian Rapids. The oarsmen panicked as they neared the white water, and cut the towline before Captain Rough gave the order. Rowing as though pursued by demons, they soon reached the safety of the Canadian shore.

The derelict schooner gathered momentum as she approached the rapids. An American ensign fluttered from her bowsprit and the British Union Jack waved proudly from her stern. Several human effigies were propped along the side rails, including a mannequin of Andrew Jackson. Roaming freely across her deck were the animals so many had come to see. The promoters had been unable or unwilling to find panthers, wildcats, or wolves. The old ship's menagerie consisted of only thirteen creatures: three bears, two foxes, one buffalo, one dog, one cat, one raccoon, and four geese. With a bear patiently climbing up one of her masts, the schooner sailed like a preposterous nineteenth century Ark toward the great deluge of Niagara.

The *Michigan* survived the first great breaker of the rapids. Her bow plunged into a trough then bounded back up on a swell, her deck awash. She was not a small vessel, however, measuring eighteen feet from her keel to her deck. Her bottom caught on submerged rocks as she negotiated the next breaker. The impact snapped her masts and cast them overboard in a tangle of rigging. Two of the bears splashed into the rapids and began to swim for Canada as the schooner swung completely around and proceeded through the rapids stern first.

The *Michigan* took on water, but remained afloat and intact as she approached the Horseshoe. A few minutes after she lost her masts she reached the brink of the great cataract, with only the buffalo still visible on her deck. She tumbled backward into the gorge and plummeted one hundred eighty feet to the surface of the lower river. The impact completely shattered her old hull. "I went below the falls immediately after the descent," one witness wrote later, "and the river exhibited a singular appearance from the thousands of fragments, there being scarcely to be seen any two boards nailed together, and many of her timbers were broken into atoms."

Of the thirteen animals aboard the *Michigan*, only four survived. The two bears that had abandoned the ship reached shore safely and were recaptured. Two of the geese survived the plunge over the Horseshoe without injury. The rest of the menagerie were not seen again. In the years following the old schooner's final voyage, souvenir hawkers at Niagara Falls sold fans and Indian headdresses made, they claimed, with feathers from the *Michigan* geese.

The animals so cruelly employed for entertainment at Niagara in 1827 were not the first to pass over the falls, nor would they be the last. The carcasses of wild animals had always appeared in the lower river, especially at the Whirlpool. The animals aboard the *Michigan* were, however, the first creatures known to have been intentionally cast over the falls. The stunt served as a model for cruel and ignorant men for another one hundred years.

Dog owners began throwing their unwanted pets into the American Rapids as early as 1836. In 1838, this item appeared in the *Lockport Democrat*:

Over the Falls, and alive.—A gentleman who resides at Niagara Falls informs us, that sometime during the winter a dog was thrown into the rapids, and was carried over the American Fall. He has occasionally been seen from the opposite side, under the high bank upon this side, and within a few days has been recovered by his master. His subsistence for several months must have been upon the bodies of animals that have gone over the falls and floated to the shore.

In 1852, a man named C. E. Shaw tied together the feet and head of his ill-tempered bulldog, "Dick," and pitched him into the river above the American Fall. Shaw watched long enough to make sure Dick went over the brink, then paid a visit to a friend. When Shaw returned to his home two hours later, he found Dick waiting for him. The surly bulldog had not only survived the awful plunge, but freed himself of his bonds. Shaw was so moved by the experience that he vowed to keep Dick until he died of old age.

Bossy at the brink of the American Fall near Prospect Point.

Dogs were not the only animals to defy the power of Niagara in the nineteenth century. In the summer of 1860, a cow gained considerable notoriety for her habit of wading through the American Rapids. The operator of the original Inclined Railway

118

at Prospect Point maintained a pasture along the riverbank upstream. His cow, affectionately known as "Bossy Simms," would often wander from the pasture to wade into the swift, but shallow water near the brink of the American Fall. On at least one occasion she ventured from Prospect Point to Goat Island. Bossy's antics amused her master and thrilled tourists, but local businessmen held a different view. To them, the cow was an embarrassment. The sight of the beast nonchalantly chewing her cud at the Brink of Doom infuriated them. They had expended a great deal of energy dramatizing the danger and power of the falls to visitors, only to see them mocked by a cow.

On August 8, 1886, William Potts and George Hazlett became the first pair of stunters to navigate the Whirlpool Rapids together in one barrel. Hazlett repeated the stunt on November 28 of the same year, this time accompanied by a young woman named Sadie Allen. Two years later, Hazlett and Potts teamed up again to plan a trip over the Horseshoe in the same sturdy barrel that had twice passed unscathed through the Whirlpool Rapids.

On Sunday, June 3, 1888, Hazlett and Potts brought their barrel to the falls for a test run. They nailed sand bags to the bottom of the huge cask for ballast and placed a live gamecock inside before sealing it. They secured the services of rivermen Dick Parker and James Greenwood, who towed the barrel out to the middle of the river and released it at about 11:30 that morning.

Thirty minutes later, the barrel dropped over the brink of the Horseshoe and vanished into the mist. It emerged intact below the fall less than a minute later. Shortly before 4:00 Hazlett and Potts recovered the barrel. One of its hoops was bent and a thick oak stave had splintered. When they opened it they discovered that the gamecock was dead, smothered by the contents of burst sandbags. Despite the damage and the mortally wounded chicken, the stunters seemed pleased with the result of their trial run. Potts announced that he would make the same trip himself on June 10.

When Carlisle Graham, the first man to run the Whirlpool Rapids in a barrel, learned of Potts's plan, he announced that *he* would go over the Horseshoe on July 4. Neither Graham nor Potts ever lived up to their promises.

Of all the tales of animal misadventure at Niagara, none is stranger than that of the runaway horse of Joe Cottella. On July 25, 1897, Cottella used a long rope to tie up his chestnut stallion to a stake in a field adjacent to an Erie Railroad warehouse on Ninth Street. At about 4:30 p.m. the horse crossed some nearby railroad tracks. When a passing train cut the rope, the horse galloped across Buffalo Avenue and down to the riverbank at Port Day.

In those days runaway horses were considered a public menace. Civic duty required that anyone who could take action to stop a runaway must do so. So it was that a group of men followed Cottella's horse down to the river, expecting to corner it there. They were surprised when the beast plunged into the water without breaking stride. They were even more surprised when he headed for the distant shore of Canada.

The horse waded through shallows and swam through deep water, passing beyond Goat Island where the swift current began to carry him toward the Canadian Rapids. Crowds of visitors watched from the island as the horse swam well beyond any hope of rescue. The following day, the *Niagara Falls Gazette* observed:

> It seemed as if the intention of the beast was to reach the green pastures of Canada to those watching him, and perhaps it was; but finally the horse was carried down to the breakers of the Horseshoe rapids, and then, instead of turning away from them the horse deliberately turned and faced them, going head foremost through the spouting and blinding spray and rapidly drawn down the roaring torrent.

Even as the horse surged through the rapids, he maintained his balance and kept trying to swim. Finally, he tumbled over a series of cascades and stopped struggling. He was either completely spent or stunned by collisions with submerged rocks. A moment later he disappeared into the gorge.

On September 7, 1901, Maud Willard intended to become famous. The twenty-five-year-old dance hall actress from Canton, Ohio, had arranged with Carlisle Graham to perform a novel double stunt in the gorge on that date. She would ride Graham's famous barrel through the Whirlpool Rapids and into the Whirlpool itself. The plan called for Graham to intercept the barrel at the head of the Devil's Hole Rapids and swim alongside it all the way to Lewiston. Willard hoped the feat would put her on the front pages of newspapers throughout the Northeast, but her hopes were soon dashed by two bullets and a dog.

On September 6, anarchist Leon Czolgosz shot President William McKinley at the Pan-American Exposition at Buffalo. The following day newspapers around the world were crowded with stories related to the shocking incident, including lengthy pieces speculating on McKinley's chances for recovery.

Any chance for Maud Willard to make the front pages of even the local papers, at least in early September, evaporated. But she and Graham had publicly vowed to perform the stunt on September 7. They decided to salvage what publicity they could by keeping their word.

At 3:40 p.m. on the appointed day, Willard crawled into Graham's barrel. For companionship she brought her pet dog. A small boat towed them to the middle of Swift Drift and released the barrel at 3:53. A trolley followed her along the tracks of the Great Gorge Route, while a motion picture camera crew aboard filmed the event. The barrel bounded through the rapids without difficulty and entered the Whirlpool at 4:04 p.m.

Maud Willard

All seemed well until the barrel made one circuit of the Whirlpool, then another without any hint that it would break free of the currents there and move into the Devil's Hole Rapids. Graham watched it from the American side of the Whirlpool until 4:45 p.m. Then he decided to make his swim without Willard. More concerned for safety than he had been in previous years, Graham wore a life preserver. He splashed into the river and swam uneventfully to Lewiston with the trolley and camera crew keeping pace.

By the time Graham returned to the Whirlpool, the sun was setting. He learned to his horror that the barrel had made at least twenty circuits of the Whirlpool but had never come close enough to shore for anyone to haul it in. Maud Willard had been trapped in the barrel for nearly five hours with only a single air hole one half inch in diameter through which to breathe.

When Graham spotted the barrel in the gathering darkness, he splashed into the river and swam for it, but the currents swept it beyond his reach. Try as he might, he could make no headway, so he returned to shore.

A searchlight car supplied by the Great Gorge Route arrived and illuminated the Whirlpool to aid a rescue party that had gathered there. A group of men led by and old riverman named Johnson finally snagged the barrel with ropes shortly before 10:00. When they pulled it up onto the rocks and opened the lid, the dog popped out like a jack-in-the-box, but Maud Willard lay motionless within. They hauled her into the open air. She was still breathing faintly, but she died minutes later, despite their efforts to resuscitate her.

Maud Willard's dog

There were many at the time who thought that Maud Willard's dog had killed his mistress by corking the barrel's air hole with his nose. While he breathed freely through the small aperture, they speculated, she slowly suffocated. Even if the dog did not do this, he certainly consumed enough oxygen in the barrel to hasten Willard's demise. Of course, had Graham abandoned his swim and instead devoted his energies to recovering the barrel, his partner might have lived to stunt another day.

Sometime during the night of March 15, 1908, a great flock of wild swans floated into the Canadian Rapids. Unable to extricate themselves from the churning water, they passed over the Horseshoe. The following morning groups of club-wielding men ventured out onto the ice bridge from Canada and killed scores of the dazed birds.

News of the slaughter was greeted with condemnation and outrage on the American side of the river. Buffalo sportsmen complained to Game Protector William C. Hodge. One prominent Buffalonian, attorney Charles L. Bullymore, wrote a letter to Hodge demanding that he conduct an investigation. Hodge did so, and promptly reported his findings to Bullymore:

> Dear Sir—Have investigated the slaughter of swans and find the following to be the facts:
>
> A flock of about 150 were on the Niagara River above the falls and were carried over the cataract and most of them were killed, maimed, and wounded. Canadians killed and captured 102 and the rest of the flock were able to escape.
>
> The slaughter was strictly in accordance with Canadian law, which permits duck shooting until the last of April. Much as all right-minded sportsmen and fair-thinking persons deprecate such things, we cannot help ourselves. The mitigating circumstance is that many were badly crippled. By the way, this is no unusual occurrence, happening every spring to a certain extent, not only with swans, but with other water fowl. But I have never before known of so large a flock of swans and so great a killing at one time.
>
> WILLIAM C. HODGE
> Game Protector

Early on March 24, 1931, three dogs were frolicking on Green Island when one fell into the American Rapids. The dog, a young German Shepherd, saved himself from drowning, but ended up trapped on an ice-glazed rock two hundred feet from the brink of the American Fall.

Crowds of tourists gathered at Prospect Point to watch the dog. One bystander telephoned the Niagara Falls Fire Department for assistance. Fire Chief George A. Wood refused to take any action until he had consulted with Tracy Levee, Chief of the Reservation Police.

Levee was inclined to do nothing. "I personally believe that it might be well to let him stay there until tomorrow," he said, "and then he may leave the rock and make his own way out of danger." He quickly altered his opinion under pressure from the mayor, the fire chief, and the public. At 1:30 p.m. he reluctantly authorized a rescue attempt, but decided to use his own men.

Kenneth Haag and Clarence Hillman, both Reservation employees, tied themselves together with a length of rope and waded through knee-deep water from Green Island to Robinson Island. From that point they reentered the shallow rapids and stepped carefully along the slick river bottom toward the stranded dog.

When the dog saw them, he left his rocky perch and walked toward them through shallow water. Haag and Hillman were almost close enough to the animal to reach out and grab him by the collar when he suddenly wheeled about and leaped back over the rock, splashing into swifter, deeper currents. He narrowly escaped being swept away before scrambling back to the security of his rock.

Haag and Hillman reached the animal a few minutes later and tied a rope to his collar. They guided him through the rapids back to Robinson Island, carrying him a good part of the way. When they brought the dog ashore, scores of spectators at Prospect Point and on Green Island cheered.

Later that day, Reservation police returned the German Shepherd to his owner, Andrew Romney. The lucky dog's name was "Jerry."

Several months after Jerry's close call, another German Shepherd ended up in the American Rapids off Prospect Point. July 3, 1931, promised to be another sweltering day in the hot spell that plagued western New York and southern Ontario. The temperature reached 80 degrees Fahrenheit by 9:00 a.m.

Many visitors to Prospect Park that morning noticed a large German Shepherd wandering along the riverbank. He had been there since at least 7:00. No one paid much attention to him, however, until he jumped into the river, apparently to cool off. He splashed about at the fringe of the rapids, then returned to shore to shake himself dry. The dog was soon back in the river. Time and again he came ashore only to return to the water. A concerned tourist went to the office of Reservation Police Chief Levee and reported the dog's behavior.

The memory of Jerry's plight was still fresh in Levee's mind. He decided to send someone to secure the dog before another rescue became necessary. Levee directed Roy Baney, a Reservation janitor, to tie the dog up until his owner could be found.

Baney found a coil of stout cord and proceeded to the riverbank. He had no difficulty tying the cord around the animal's neck, but he was unable to hold him. The dog bolted and snapped the cord. His momentum carried him far out into the river. The current immediately bowled him over and swept him over the brink of the American Fall. No one expected to see the dog again.

Incredibly, the big German Shepherd survived the plunge without injury. John Kavanaugh, a Cave of the Winds guide, saw the dog swimming among driftwood in a pool below the fall. Kavanaugh climbed over the railing of the wooden catwalks at the edge of the fall and hauled him to safety.

A police officer takes Jerry into custody.

On September 18, 1984, C. J. Ann, a subway dispatcher from Seoul, South Korea, visited the Cave of the Winds. With him were K. W. Bae and Carlos Tydingco Jr. Ann and his companions were standing on the wooden "Hurricane Deck" at the base of the Bridal Veil Fall when something hurtled out of the spray from above, slammed into the planking beneath them, and caromed into Ann's leg. Instantly, the water swirling about their feet turned red.

"I saw blood over my right leg," Ann later told *Niagara Gazette* reporter Nancy Tracewell. "I thought, *I am bleeding.* Then I am very surprised."

The blood on the Hurricane Deck was not Ann's, but that of a large Chinook salmon that now wriggled feebly on the planking. A Cave of the Winds guide disposed of the fish by kicking it off the Hurricane Deck, but Ann wanted to keep it as a souvenir. He climbed over the railing and retrieved it from the rocks below. The salmon proved to be worth keeping: it was two feet long and weighed almost fifteen pounds. Had it struck him directly, Ann might have been seriously injured or killed.

Reflecting on his encounter with the fish, Ann later said, "It was very enjoyful."

12

WE CAN ONLY DIE ONCE

O, I have passed a miserable night,
So full of ugly sights, of ghastly dreams,
That, as I am a Christian faithful man,
I would not spend another such a night,
Though 't were to buy a world of happy days.

—*William Shakespeare*

In the summer of 1918, preparations were underway to divert more water from the upper Niagara to the hydroelectric generating stations downriver. On August 6, a scalding hot, humid day, tugboats of the Great Lakes Dredge & Dock Company were moving equipment engaged in deepening the channel at the head of the Hydraulic Canal at Port Day. Dredging platform crews scooped up sand and muck from the riverbed and dumped it into eighty-by-thirty foot steel scows.

At 3:00 that afternoon, the tug *Hassayampa* was hauling a scow toward the dredging site off Port Day when Captain J. Wallace overlooked a sandbar and ran aground. The *Hassayampa* listed badly and was unable to free herself. Captain Enos White of the tug *Mayer* came to the rescue immediately, as did Captain Charles Smith of the *Kinch*. The tugs *Cowles* and *Helen M.* idled nearby to assist, if necessary. The *Mayer* and the *Kinch* took positions alongside the *Hassayampa* and quickly righted her, but the sudden strain on the three tow cables holding the scow against the swift currents of the Niagara proved too much: the cables parted and the scow began to drift downstream. None of the tugs was able to intercept the scow or cast a line to her. She was too far away, and the river too swift.

Manning the scow were two Buffalonians, James H. Harris, a 53-year-old rigger, and 51-year-old Gustave Ferdinand Lofberg, a native of Sweden. Lofberg, a bachelor, had sailed for more than thirty-five years at sea and on the Great Lakes. Harris had been with the company for only a month. He was married and had five children.

Harris and Lofberg were working on deck in the stifling heat when the *Hassayampa* went aground. They had no idea anything was amiss until the whistles of the five tugs upstream began to shriek the alarm. By that time the current had carried them into the Canadian Channel.

Lofberg quickly surveyed the situation. They were gathering speed, heading inexorably toward the rapids above the Horseshoe. "Look," he said to Harris. "We're going over the falls. By God, we're lost." The Swede tried to remain calm. If I must die, he thought, why, I must. That's all.

Lofberg wasn't going to die without a fight, however. He had once been adrift on a barge in a Lake Superior gale. He had stubbornly survived forty-eight hours of battering in that storm and had seen a fellow deckhand carried to oblivion by the angry lake. He wouldn't give up easily, no matter how certain he might be of the outcome.

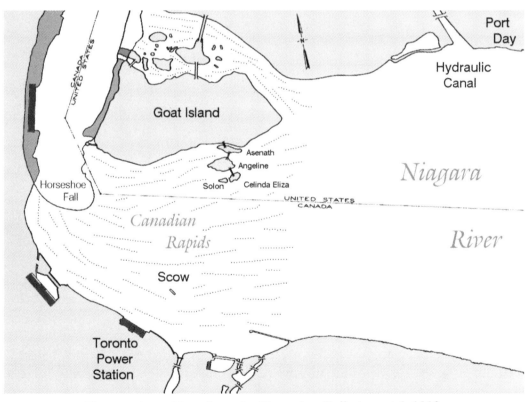

The scow's position above the Horseshoe Fall, August 6, 1918.

He wasted no time, but set about stopping the scow's progress toward the fall. At the stern of the vessel rested a six-ton concrete anchor that he and Harris quickly loosed. When the massive block splashed into the river it slowed the scow, but only for a moment. The vessel plowed on through the rapids, dragging the anchor over the smooth riverbed.

"We are going over!" Harris shouted.

"We can only die once," Lofberg remarked.

Suddenly the scow ground to a halt on a rock shelf. The men fastened a cable to a cargo roller and dropped it into the river. With any luck this makeshift anchor would help secure their position, but the fierce rapids about them threatened to dislodge the scow. Lofberg could think of only one more thing to do. He and Harris immediately went to work opening the vessel's watertight compartments. Once the compartments were flooded the scow rested more solidly on the river bottom than before. Even so, it swayed and lurched as the great green waves and whitecaps rolled by.

The scow, as seen from the western flank of the Toronto Power Station.

Lofberg and Harris were marooned 850 feet from the Canadian shore a little more than half a mile above the brink of the Horseshoe Fall.

No sooner had the *Hassayampa*'s tow lines parted, than word of impending tragedy spread. Crowds had gathered along the shore on both sides of the river to watch the scow's passage. Ross Coddington, superintendent of dredging for the Hydraulic Power Company, arrived at Port Day just as Harris and Lofberg drifted into the Canadian Rapids. Coddington telephoned the fire departments in Niagara Falls, New York, and Niagara Falls, Ontario. He also called the United States Coast Guard stations at Buffalo and Youngstown. Rescue operations were soon underway.

Lofberg and Harris trapped in the Canadian Rapids.

Assistant Chief Richard Miller of the Niagara Falls, New York, Fire Department rushed to the Toronto Power Station on the Canadian shore. Miller, accompanied by a squad of men from his headquarters, quickly set up a tiny cannon and fired a lifeline toward the grounded scow. Thousands of onlookers cheered lustily when the gun barked in the thick air. The cheer abruptly faded to a groan: the grapnel at the end of the lifeline fell into the rapids less than halfway to the scow.

The Great War was still raging in Europe so there were plenty of Canadian soldiers on hand to guard the power plants along the Ontario shore against sabotage. A handful of these men joined Canadian firefighters under the command of Chief A. H. Newman. They attempted unsuccessfully to float wooden benches to the scow by means of ropes secured at a point upriver.

Meanwhile, a rescue team assembled at the Coast Guard station at Youngstown. Captain A. D. Nelson, U.S.C., commandeered a truck belonging to the Army Quartermaster Corps. At Nelson's direction, Private John Trotter, an Army garage mechanic, removed the governor from the big truck's engine. At 4:15 P.M. Nelson, a Coast Guard lifesaving crew, and a contingent of American soldiers piled into the truck with huge coils of hemp rope, a breeches buoy, and a brass rescue cannon. Nelson selected Private Fred Daubney to drive.

It was little more than fifteen miles from Youngstown to Niagara Falls, but a detour around the dilapidated Lewiston Hill Road added ten miles to the trip. Daubney drove like a madman, however, and covered the twenty-five miles of dirt and gravel roads in less than thirty-five minutes.

The instant the truck arrived at the Toronto Power Station, Nelson's men began unloading their equipment. At 5:00 the cannon was in position. Nelson sighted the gun in on the scow and, at 5:05, yanked the lanyard. For the second time that day cannon fire sounded at the falls. For the second time that day the crowd of thousands began to cheer, but this time the cheering continued unabated for many minutes. Nelson's aim had been perfect: 1,500 feet of lifeline arced out over the Canadian Rapids and fell dead center across the scow.

Lofberg and Harris were ready for the lifeline when it dropped amidships. They had worked themselves nearly to exhaustion preparing for just such a rescue attempt. They had modified a winch running the length of the vessel to create a windlass for hauling in ropes. They quickly secured the lifeline to the mechanism.

At the shore end of the line, Nelson directed a gang of volunteers to take up the slack and keep it from sagging into the rapids. Policemen, soldiers, civilians, and firemen grabbed the line with eager hands and hauled it up to the roof of the Toronto Power Station. There Nelson and his Coast Guardsmen secured an inch-thick rope to the lifeline along with a block and tackle holding a double guy line. Three groups of volunteers—nearly one hundred men in all—held the lines taut while Lofberg and Harris winched the rigging toward the scow.

The work on both ends of the line was hellish. The men ashore labored in the draft of the power station cooling vents in temperatures that shot above one hundred degrees Fahrenheit. On the scow, Lofberg and Harris alternated shifts at the winch. Each full turn of the crank brought the heavy lines only three inches closer to the scow. For more than three hours they ratcheted the winch. When at last the block and tackle came aboard they were on the verge of collapse. They lashed the heavy rope to a cleat and secured the block and tackle. Nelson had written instructions to them in indelible ink on a piece of wood attached to the end of the line. They read the message then signaled success by waving their arms.

Nelson's volunteers passed the rope over the roof of the power station station and lashed it to trees on the grounds below. It was dusk when the Coast Guardsmen secured the guy ropes and prepared the breeches buoy, a canvas seat slung from a pulley mounted on the inch-thick rope.

Captain Nelson (fourth from left) with his men.

Fred Huebner, chief electrician at the scene, rigged a battery of 4,000 watt searchlights on the roof of the power station. He kept their beams on the scow and rapids as darkness settled. The lights remained on all night.

At 9:30 Nelson's men began to work the guy ropes to haul the breeches buoy out to the scow. As the buoy moved out over the water one of the guy ropes sagged until it hung in the rapids. The twenty-mile-per-hour current dragged the rope downstream where it caught among rocks on the riverbed. The men hauled the other guy line to free it and once again tried to advance the buoy, with the same result. Time and again the Coast Guardsmen hauled on one guy line, only to watch as the other line sagged into the rapids.

Someone cut huge letters out of sheets of cardboard and held them in front of the searchlights to spell out messages to Lofberg and Harris. One of the first messages they sent was, "LINE IS FOULED." Nelson knew the men on the scow could read the messages when he instructed them to "PULL IN ON SMALL LINE." Lofberg and Harris obeyed immediately.

For two hours Nelson's men and the men on the scow hauled back and forth on the guy lines, but they never moved the buoy more than 250 feet from shore. Just before midnight Nelson decided to postpone the rescue until morning. He ordered this message sent to the scow: "REST."

Some of the men along the shore began to doubt that Lofberg and Harris would be rescued. A similar scene had been played out 65 years earlier when another scow deckhand named Joseph Avery became trapped in the American Rapids. He spent more than twenty hours clinging to a rock while a throng of workmen attempted five times to rescue him. Ropes, pulleys, boats, and gritty human determination had all failed then: the last rescue boat inadvertently knocked Avery into the water. He plunged over the American Fall with a shriek heard half a mile away.

It didn't look good for Lofberg and Harris. They had been hard at work for nine hours in 85 degree heat and high humidity on a vessel tottering at the brink of doom. Their existence had settled into mindless drudgery accompanied by fear that at any moment the river would dislodge the scow and carry them over the Horseshoe Fall. Despite her anchors and flooded compartments, the big vessel yawed and pitched incessantly. And there was always the possibility that the men ashore would pull her from the rock ledge with the rescue line.

The men on the scow knew they had to sleep—rest was essential if they were to be of any use in assisting in their own rescue the next day. They balled their coats into pillows and stretched out in the stern.

Lofberg plummeted into sleep, but he woke with a start almost immediately; the scow had lurched, making him think they were going over the fall. He fell back asleep, but the scow moved again and he woke. Harris suffered in the same manner. Again and again the exhausted men nodded off only to scramble out of sleep in a panic when the deck heaved beneath them. After hours of trying, they gave up any hope of rest. They turned their attentions, instead, to planning their salvation when the river finally had its way with the scow.

Harris lashed sixteen feet of rope to a barrel and tied a noose at the free end. He had no intention of taking the plunge over the Horseshoe with the scow. When the time came he would tighten the noose around his waist and cast the barrel overboard then jump in after it. He was content—perhaps amused—with the idea of going over the fall on the *outside* of a barrel.

Lofberg, the more experienced sailor, thought his best chance of survival was to stay with his ship. He was prepared to lash himself to an eye bolt in one of the vessel's cargo pockets. He ran a length of tow line through the eye and arranged the line so he could wrap it around his body several times.

At 2:00 A.M. Lofberg looked at his watch, then at Harris. "Well, if we're going to go over the Falls," he said testily, "I wish the thing would happen!"

Both men were drenched with sweat and spray and the night had turned cold. They were hungry, tired, and miserable.

Back at the power station, Nelson was frustrated. When the guy line broke around midnight, he was faced with the bleak prospect of sending his men back to Youngstown to gather more rope. He could come up with no better idea than to start from scratch and shoot a second lifeline to the scow. While he was considering his next step, a slim, redheaded young man named Hill approached him and volunteered to untangle the guy lines.

William "Red" Hill was a Canadian riverman with at least two rescues to his credit. He had saved a woman from a burning house in 1895 and had helped haul stragglers from the Niagara Gorge during the Ice Bridge Tragedy of February 1912. He wasn't in top form, however. He had been gassed during his recent army service in Europe and was still recuperating.

Nelson accepted Hill's offer.

A little after 3:00 a.m. Hill slipped into the buoy and hauled himself across the rapids with the help of Ontario Power Company riggers working the guy lines. About halfway to the scow he found a jammed block. He freed the block and returned to shore. But there was still something wrong; the guy lines did not work properly. At 5:30 a.m. he went back out, this time to within 150 feet of the scow. There he found that one of the guy ropes had wrapped around the main line. He untangled the mess then waved his arms. Riggers Charles Fossett and Thomas Dorrington hauled him back to the power station roof.

At last the lines were clear. Shortly after 8:00 a.m. the riggers moved the breeches buoy to the scow without a hitch.

Harris and Lofberg looked down at the waiting breeches buoy. "You go ahead, Jim," Lofberg said. "I'll stay behind and man the ropes because I know how to handle them better than you." There really wasn't any rope handling for the Swede to do, but he could see that Harris was exhausted and hungry. At 8:25 Lofberg helped his companion into the buoy.

William Hill

Harris did not have the strength to ride high in the mechanism. His legs dangled limply from the canvas seat and the lifeline sagged toward the rapids. As the men ashore began to pull him to safety Harris sagged lower and lower until his legs were in the water. Several times he was swamped and nearly drowned, but he could do nothing to pull himself up—he had only strength enough to keep his head above water or hold his breath. After what seemed an eternity he rose from the churning river and moved up the inclined rope to the power station roof.

Nelson's men and the riggers began to cheer. Thousands of spectators along the shore on both sides of the river knew then that at least one of the deckhands was safe. They, too, began to cheer.

At 8:50 Harris reached the power station. There Nelson's volunteers removed him from the buoy. Doctors were on hand to examine him, but he needed only rest.

Lofberg comes ashore, as seen from the eastern flank of the power station.

"I'm going back on land somewhere and lash myself to a tree," Harris told his rescuers. "Then I'll know I'm safe." But he didn't look for a tree. Instead, he walked on rubbery legs to the edge of the roof and gazed out at the scow where Lofberg awaited his turn. Harris was clearly intent on seeing the drama to its end, but Nelson's volunteers persuaded him to leave. When they led him through the main door of the power station station a wildly cheering crowd greeted him. His guardians hustled him into a waiting car and drove him to the Cataract House, a sprawling hotel on the American side of the river.

The excitement on the roof caused a delay in the riggers' activities and nearly an hour passed before they could get the buoy back to the scow. At 9:45 Lofberg lowered himself into the canvas seat. Unlike Harris, he had strength enough to grasp the pulley mechanism and keep himself out of the water. The Swede rode high for the entire trip back to shore. He crossed the rapids in five minutes and scarcely got his feet wet. Despite his fatigue he smiled broadly when he set foot on the power station roof and immediately began looking for someone with a spare plug of chewing tobacco. Ross Coddington and Red Hill were among the first to greet him.

Lofberg

Harris

Lofberg, too, was whisked off to a car and soon joined Harris on the verandah of the Cataract House. The deckhands posed for photographs and talked with reporters.

"Lofberg was certainly game on that barge," Harris said in response to one newsman's question. "He kept up my courage with his repeated assurances that we would be saved. He is the gamest man I ever saw." He went on to give his account of the events of the previous day and night.

Lofberg talked at some length about his thoughts and actions while on the barge. "I hope I shall be spared such another night of torture and suffering," he concluded.

That afternoon Lofberg and Harris went to their bunks aboard a dredging platform at the head of the Hydraulic Canal. They slept as though dead, but arose the next morning and reported for work as if nothing unusual had happened.

Officials of the Great Lakes Dredge and Dock Company briefly considered a salvage operation to recover the $60,000 scow, but the vessel's position in the river made such a proposition too dangerous and expensive.

The river never did have its way with the scow. A year passed, then another and another, but the scow remained lodged in the rapids. Decades passed. In 1947 a portion of the hull broke away and vanished in the boiling green river, but the bulk of the vessel remained. In 1961 the scow played a role in one of the great tragedies in Niagara's history when two men and two women plunged into the Canadian Rapids when their boat capsized. Witnesses saw one of the men climb aboard the scow in an effort to save himself. He fell inside the rusted hulk and was not seen again. Two of his companions went over the Horseshoe. One died in a power plant intake.

The scow that in 1918 was the scene of high drama and courage has now been in the river for more than eighty years. Defiant as ever, she shows no sign of going anywhere soon.

13

UNLIKELY HEROES

When a man from our midst does a heroic act for applause, his views differ from those of him who endangers and risks his life for a fellow man, not for the sake of public notoriety and applause, but from the guidance of his heart. Such is my idea of a hero.

—Charles E. Cromley

Arguably, there are two types of hero. One masters his fear for the benefit of others; the second, perhaps fearless, seeks the praise and adoration of the masses through acts of daring. Virgil's humble Aeneas and Homer's vain Odysseus are classical representatives of the types. Examples from our own era might include Norman Schwartzkopf, who braved a Vietnamese minefield to rescue fallen soldiers, and Evel Knievel, whose spectacular motorcycle stunts thrilled millions. One hero gauges success by the number of lives saved, while another measures it by the volume of the applause and the girth of his wallet. The history of Niagara abounds with the exploits of policemen, firefighters, barrel riders, and funambulists who exemplify both. There is, however, a third type of hero.

Witnesses to impending tragedy frequently feel an urge to intervene, to alter the outcome of events, but reason and fear usually prevent them from taking action. Niagara has been the scene of an untold number of fatal accidents and suicides that might have been prevented, had only one or two persons emerged from the throngs of tourists and gawkers to take action. But not every suicide at Niagara has succeeded, nor has every accident been fatal. Often enough, untrained women and men step from the crowd and distinguish themselves by averting tragedy. These heroes, great and humble, have sprung from every station in society. Most have been good people. At least one was a scoundrel.

In 1878, the village of Niagara Falls, New York, had no more disreputable citizen than Pypus Walker. "Py" Walker was a 29-year-old fisherman who earned extra money by ferrying passengers across the upper Niagara. He lived with his wife and two small children in a tiny stone and frame house near Port Day. Walker might have been a valued member of the community and respected family man had he not suffered from three glaring character defects: he loved to drink, he could not resist a bet, and he hated competition.

Py Walker routinely drank himself into a stupor, and made no secret of his liquor consumption. It would have been difficult to find an adult in the vicinity who had not seen him staggering about on shore or—if it can be imagined—staggering about in his boat. Few in his day knew the upper Niagara as well as he did when intoxicated. When he was sober, his skill as a boatman and knowledge of the river were unsurpassed. He liked to best the unsuspecting in wagers by rowing to the head of Goat Island—a feat considered insane by most rivermen. Sometimes he would make the trip just for the hell of it.

Walker was a rogue, even as rivermen go, and was widely reputed to be a smuggler and a saboteur. He had a fondness for cutting the mooring lines of boats left unattended by his competitors. The river would then carry these forlorn vessels over the falls. Fishermen, rumrunners, and ferrymen were all nervous whenever he was in the neighborhood.

Despite his many flaws, Py Walker was not all bad. Over the course of his brief, turbulent career he rescued as many as twenty people from drowning or going over the falls.

A strong northwest wind blew throughout the day on August 9, 1878. The river was running rough and, with the coaxing wind, more rapidly toward the falls. The weather did not deter Jim Geagan and Fred Burdick from setting out from the American shore in a sailboat belonging to Burdick's family. The two young men headed for Chippawa with Geagan at the helm. Just beyond Grass Island he handed control of the boat to Burdick.

Suddenly, the sail jibbed, causing the boat to heel so violently that it took on water. The sail then jibbed again and the river swamped the tiny craft.

Geagan and Burdick found handholds on the hull and tried to set the sail to maneuver themselves back to shore. The effort ended when the boat rolled over on its side. They tried then to climb up onto the keel, but the boat rolled again and pitched them back into the river. They were drifting helplessly toward the Canadian Rapids.

Burdick removed his shoes and socks and swam for shore. Geagan stayed with the boat, shouting and waving his hat to attract attention. At one point he thought rescue was imminent when another sailboat set out from Port Day and headed toward him. The sailboat changed course, however. No one aboard had seen Geagan or the wrecked boat, now moving inexorably toward the Horseshoe.

Geagan had almost given up hope when he saw another boat leave Port Day. It was a light skiff with a solitary figure at the oars—Py Walker. He saw it turn downstream in hot pursuit of Burdick, who had failed to reach Grass Island and was now perilously close to the American Rapids.

The boatman intercepted Burdick and hauled him aboard. Then he came about and rowed for Geagan. A few minutes later, Geagan climbed into the boat with the help of Walker.

Walker plucked Geagan from the river only a few hundred feet above the Canadian Rapids. His safest course would then have been to make for Goat Island, the nearest landing. He rowed, instead, for the American mainland with swift, powerful strokes. With the strength and skill that was the envy of all rivermen, he propelled the skiff through treacherous waters back to Port Day. Burdick's boat plunged over the Horseshoe a short time later.

A hero's welcome awaited Walker on shore. For a day his fellow citizens sang his praises. Even the *Niagara Falls Gazette* joined in the chorus, stating, "Walker's efforts in saving the two young men constituted one of the most daring and brave deeds ever performed on the river."

It was quickly apparent to everyone, however, that Walker had not changed his character. He had merely displayed a paradoxical aspect of it. Within days, Pypus Walker the hero was forgotten, replaced by the familiar personality of Py Walker the misfit.

Less than a year after saving Burdick and Geagan, Py Walker found himself in need of rescue. On May 25, 1879, he began the day as he often did—by cracking open a bottle. By 2:00 p.m., he was so intoxicated he could barely walk. He took his bottle of liquor in hand and headed for the river. His wife pleaded with him to stay ashore, but he dismissed her.

Walker climbed into his skiff and rowed out to Grass Island. There he enjoyed several glasses of beer with his cronies before stumbling back into the skiff. He shoved off again and headed out into the river about two miles above the American Fall. No one knows if he intended to land on Goat Island or return to Port Day. Walker was so drunk that he may not have known himself.

A few minutes after he left Grass Island, Walker entered the American Rapids. In his inebriated state he may have decided to challenge the river as he had never before challenged it. Perhaps he had merely fallen asleep at the oars.

A number of men ashore saw Walker's plight and began shouting. He was in the main channel of the rapids, but there was still hope that he could guide his craft into the shallows. A few witnesses recognized the man in the boat. They knew that if anyone could survive this stretch of river, it was Py Walker. They yelled and pointed toward the sluiceway near the Cataract House, a hotel overlooking the rapids.

Walker began to row. It looked as though he would reach the safety of the sluiceway until one of his oars unexpectedly "caught a crab"—struck a submerged rock—and popped out of its lock. He fumbled to save the oar, but it slipped overboard.

Walker could think of nothing better to do, so he stood and took a final gulp from his bottle. As the skiff lurched through the rapids, he fell into the bow. He did not get up again.

Miraculously, the skiff grounded on a rock at the fringe of the rapids just above the Goat Island Bridge. There it teetered and spun in water shallow enough for a man to stand in and await rescue. Walker was oblivious to this chance for survival, however, and lay sprawled at the bottom of the boat.

"There was something peculiarly horrifying in the apathy of the endangered man," the *Buffalo Daily Courier* observed the following day. "But as an eyewitness remarked, he acted like all drunken men: he was down and he didn't care very much whether he went over the falls or not. But the spectators did care, and they stood in sickening surprise watching for the catastrophe which was evidently so close at hand. At length it came."

An eddy dumped the skiff back into the torrent. The small boat quickly accelerated and plowed into a rock. The impact split the hull as efficiently as a monstrous ax. Walker scrambled onto a fragment of the bow and lay there, as one witness put it, "like an oyster on its half shell." A moment later he plummeted over the American Fall and disappeared among the great rocks and blazing white foam, never to be seen again.

The brief, but conspicuous career of Pypus Walker had come to an untimely end. His heroism, perhaps the sole redeeming feature of an otherwise sociopathic personality, was briefly mourned and promptly forgotten.

It is not surprising that most of Niagara's heroes have been young men. Young men generally have the strength, endurance, and daring to effect a rescue under the right circumstances. Youth, however, is not a prerequisite for heroism. Consider this item from the *Buffalo Evening News* of September 11, 1891:

IN THE MAD WATER
A Man and Woman End Their
Lives at Niagara Falls

DELIBERATE AND DETERMINED

An Old Man Nearly Loses His Life
Trying to Save the Woman
—Their Names Not
Known

NIAGARA FALLS, N.Y., Sept. 11.—Two suicides took place at the falls yesterday afternoon, and there is more excitement here than there has been in many years. One was that of a man, the other of a woman. There was no connection between the cases, apparently, but they are shrouded in almost complete mystery, as neither left any indication of the cause impelling to suicide.

A well-dressed man, about 45 years old apparently, walked up about 2 o'clock to three strangers who were standing on Luna Island. Luna Island is on the brink of the precipice over which the river tumbles, and fairly overhangs the falls.

"What is the name of these falls?" he asked.

They told him "The American Falls."

He remarked quietly: "A man would get badly smashed going over," and walked away.

Shortly afterwards they saw him standing in the rapids by the side of the island, a few yards above the brink. One of the men called to him to save himself. He answered, "I am going over!" and threw himself or fell in the swift current and was carried over the falls.

About two hours later a young woman was sitting upon one of the benches in Prospect Park. She was about 25 years old and dressed in black. She finally arose and walked down the gravel path along the side of the river until about twenty feet from the edge of the falls. Then she turned aside and went down the incline and walked into the swirling rapids.

An old man named Heim, living in Philadelphia, was looking at the falls and saw her. Jumping the wall, he plunged into the water to save her. Battling against the current, he struggled along until he succeeded in reaching her. He seized her hand, but she jerked it from his grasp and was swept away to death.

Heim almost lost his own life as the result of his heroic effort to save an undesired life. He was in great danger of being carried after her himself, and it was only after a hard fight that he was taken from the river. Heim is about 70 years old and was exhausted by his struggle.

Neither of the suicides can be identified. The woman left a black silk umbrella with a peculiar knot-like natural wood head.

There are few young men who would consider doing what R. I. Heim did. He saw an impending tragedy, felt the urge to intervene, and stepped from the crowd. Heim was unsuccessful, but his valiant attempt to alter the outcome of events was remarkable.

Women have distinguished themselves as Niagara heroes, as well. At 6:00 p.m.

on August 7, 1897, Mrs. D. L. Zach and her daughter were taking in the sights at Prospect Point. A drunken young man suddenly climbed the parapet at the brink of the American Fall. He had one foot on the iron rail surmounting the wall, and was halfway to Eternity when several men grabbed him and hurried him off toward the office of the reservation superintendent.

The Zachs watched with interest as the men hauled their struggling captive away. The Zachs' interest soon became alarm when the young man escaped and came running back toward them.

He once again climbed the parapet, but as he sprang for the water the Zachs grabbed his coattails and began screaming for assistance. The outcome of the ensuing tug-of-war was briefly in doubt. The trio tottered at the brink of the fall until Thomas Hines, a Maid of the Mist employee, arrived at the scene and added his strength to the contest. They quickly had the youth safely on the pavement.

As soon as they had subdued him, a handful of the young man's friends arrived and led him away before Reservation Police could arrest him on a charge of public drunkenness, or worse. His identity was never learned.

Nearly a century later, another woman effected a dramatic rescue above the Canadian Rapids. On August 14, 1992, 42-year-old Herman Townsend went scuba diving in the Chippawa Channel near Grand Island. His diving partner that day was a friend, 45-year-old Joann Globus. Somehow Globus became entangled in a safety tether while she was in the water near their inflatable dinghy. While trying to free herself, she lost her air hose mouthpiece.

Townsend swam to her side and found that she wasn't breathing. Her lips were blue. He didn't know if she was drowning or had suffered a heart attack, but he knew he had to get her breathing again. He tried to administer cardiopulmonary resuscitation in the water, without effect. Minutes later he was in trouble himself.

Shortly before 1:00 p.m., Karen Schlachter, a 28-year-old special education teacher from Cleveland, was peddling her bicycle south along the Niagara Parkway between Chippawa and Fort Erie. She heard someone screaming for help, and saw the dinghy anchored in the river. Not far from the boat she saw Townsend drifting about one hundred yards from shore.

Schlachter abandoned her bicycle and ran down the grassy bank to the water's edge. She began shouting to Townsend that he was going to be all right.

Townsend repeatedly screamed that his diving partner was in trouble.

Schlachter returned to the parkway and flagged down a passing motorist. She told him to dial 911 on his cellular telephone. Then she ran along the shore to keep pace with the stricken diver. Townsend had floated into swifter currents that would soon carry him to the Canadian Rapids.

Schlachter knew that if something wasn't done quickly the man in the water would end up going over the Horseshoe Fall. She stripped off her shoes, socks, and T-shirt, and waded out into the river. When the water became too deep to wade, she began to swim.

The current was faster than she had guessed. It took ten minutes to get to Townsend. When she reached him, he was floating like a dead man. She grabbed his hand and shouted, "Hey!"

Townsend did not respond at first. He seemed to be in shock. After a moment he began to babble about his diving partner being trapped under the dinghy.

Schlachter tried to tow him, but he was difficult to move due to the weight of his diving gear. She urged him to start kicking his feet. Townsend was slow to respond, but with her prodding he finally began to move his legs. His swim fins and her vigorous strokes soon got them underway. They began to move slowly toward the Canadian shore.

When they were about one hundred fifty feet from the riverbank, Jeff Somerville arrived at the scene. Somerville, a volunteer firefighter, had been driving down the parkway when he picked up the 911 call on his radio pager. He splashed into the river and swam out to assist Schlachter. Together they hauled Townsend ashore.

Schlachter was exhausted, but otherwise unharmed. Townsend was treated for shock at a local hospital. Niagara Parks Police dispatched a boat to rescue Joann Globus, but when the crew pulled her from the water she was dead.

The Carnegie Hero Fund Commission awarded Karen Schlachter a medal and a cash grant.

On June 14, 1993, Frankie Kennedy was returning home from Toronto with his family. Kennedy, a 36-year-old plumber and volunteer firefighter from Elco, Pennsylvania, was tired and eager to get the trip over with, but his teenage nephew, Steven, begged him repeatedly to stop at Niagara Falls. Kennedy relented and took the family to Prospect Park to see the American Fall. He planned to stay for no more than half an hour, then get back on the road again.

As the family stood along the railing near Prospect Point, Kennedy's daughter, Kara, screamed suddenly. His mother then began screaming. They had spotted a woman hurtling through the rapids a few feet from shore.

Kennedy saw the woman, too. He shot a glance at his wife, Rayme.

"No!" Rayme shouted, anticipating he would do something rash. "No! No!"

Kennedy ignored his wife and hopped over the railing at a point less than fifty from the brink of the American Fall. He sprinted along the jumble of rocks at water's edge.

The woman in the water had apparently tried to commit suicide and then changed her mind. She was frantically clawing at rocks to stop her progress through the rapids.

Kennedy intercepted her about fifteen feet from the fall. He made a desperate grab for her, but missed. The current swept her around a bush at the shoreline. She disappeared. Kennedy sprang downstream to try again, but he couldn't see her. For an instant he thought she had gone over the fall. Suddenly he saw her pink socks in the water. She had apparently slowed herself by clutching at the bush's roots.

Kennedy dived onto the flat rocks less than ten feet from the brink and stretched as far out into the river as he could. He extended his hand, caught the woman by the arm, and held on tight.

By this time, Kennedy's father, Raymond, and his nephew had climbed the railing. They were joined by two "Deadheads," Jason Roy and Tom Newman, in town for a Grateful Dead concert. The four newcomers grabbed Frankie by the legs and prevented the woman's momentum from carrying them both over the fall. They quickly pulled Frankie and the woman out of danger.

The name of the 36-year-old woman Frankie Kennedy saved was never made public, though authorities later confirmed that she had, indeed, attempted to kill herself. She was depressed after her recent divorce, and had spent the month preceding her suicide attempt living in a car. Eight months after the rescue she sent Kennedy a small Bible and a four page letter expressing her thanks.

Kennedy's feat made the front pages of newspapers in New York, Ontario, and Pennsylvania.

"I think everyone is making too much of this," he later said of the publicity surrounding his selfless act. "You can only do what you can do. That's what I did."

In 1994 the Carnegie Hero Fund Commission awarded Frankie Kennedy a medal commemorating his bravery.

Courageous acts at Niagara Falls demonstrate that heroism is not confined to one gender, or to youth, or to a privileged class, or even to decent people.

"When it comes to the pinch," George Orwell once wrote, "human beings are heroic."

14

THE REAL McCLOY

An airy crowd came rushing where he stood,
Which fill'd the margin of the fatal flood:
Husbands and wives, boys and unmarried maids,
And mighty heroes' more majestic shades,
And youths, intomb'd before their fathers' eyes,
With hollow groans, and shrieks, and feeble cries.

—Virgil

In 1873 Captain Matthew Webb dived from the steamship *Russia* during a gale, in a futile effort to rescue a shipmate. This selfless act made him famous in his native England. Two years later he became the first person to swim the English Channel. That exploit won him $20,000 in prize money and made his name familiar to newspaper readers around the world.

All media sensations fade, and so it was with Captain Webb. It is, perhaps, for this reason he decided to reestablish his fame with another spectacular feat: he would swim the Whirlpool Rapids.

Newspaper reporters and Frederick Kyle, Webb's manager, led him to believe that several railroad companies would pay a $10,000 prize for the swim. They convinced him that the railroads were eager to sell tickets for excursion trains that would convey tens of thousands of spectators to watch him. In June of 1883 he announced his intentions, but he soon learned that the railroad owners wanted nothing to do with what they felt was a suicidal stunt. There was no prize money and there would be no excursion trains. Webb decided to do it anyway to salvage his reputation.

On July 24, 1883, Captain Webb arranged to have ferryman John McCloy row him out into the river above the Whirlpool Rapids. Shortly before 4:00 p.m., Webb went to McCloy's house in the gorge near the Canadian Maid of the Mist landing. He chatted with Lizzie McCloy while waiting for her husband to return from a trip to the American side of the river. She asked him if he thought he would ever see his family again.

"I hope to," Webb replied. He had a wife and two young children.

John McCloy arrived moments later in his rowboat. Webb, perhaps for luck, kissed the McCloys' infant daughter, Nettie, before climbing into the boat.

It would take McCloy about ten minutes to get to the point at which Webb planned to enter the water. As he rowed, he struck up a conversation with his passenger after the ages-old custom of cabbies and ferrymen. "Have you swum often?"

"Many times," Webb said.

"Have you ever seen the rapids?"

"I've had a glimpse of them."

McCloy knew that Webb had swum the English Channel. He boldly asked him how much of the prize money remained.

"About fifteen thousand dollars."

McCloy had a very good idea what the river had in store for his passenger, so he told Webb to forget the swim and go ashore to spend some of that money.

Webb ignored the suggestion.

It was not quite 4:30 p.m. when they entered Swift Drift, the calm water just above the rapids. McCloy urged Webb one last time to return to shore.

Webb responded by stripping down to his red cotton swimming trunks.

"Now don't you jump out of the stern of this boat," McCloy cautioned. "I don't want you to tip it over."

"Never fear," Webb said. "I don't want to take you along with me." He stood at McCloy's feet in the center of the boat and dived overboard. He swam toward the rapids with graceful, confident strokes.

McCloy watched him briefly, then rowed to safety.

A bricklayer named Richard Turner found Webb's body in a cove near Lewiston four days later. That same day, *The Saturday Review* of London described Webb's fatal swim as "a piece of criminal rashness." The magazine voiced an opinion of Webb embraced by many:

> The utmost he entitled himself to is the contemptuous pity which may be properly felt for a brave man who has been turned to foolishness by vulgar applause, and who threw his life away for the ignoble object of pleasing a mob, and getting talked about in the newspapers.

Captain Matthew Webb was buried at Oakwood Cemetery in Niagara Falls, New

York, on July 30, 1883.

John McCloy enjoyed his first taste of fame on the occasion of Webb's last. In the summer of 1883 newspapers in North America and Great Britain quoted him extensively in connection with Webb's death, but he was only a bit player in the Englishman's tragedy. He is remembered today, if at all, as the man who rowed Webb to his doom.

John "Jack" McCloy was born in Chippawa, Ontario, on March 4, 1851. He grew up on the banks of the Niagara and in his youth was trained as a machinist. In 1870, he set out to leave his mark on the world—"to make a record," as he often said. He joined the First Ontario Rifles and served in the Northwest Territories. When he left the army he kicked about and worked odd jobs. In 1877 he returned to Niagara and took a position with the Prospect Park Company as a tour guide.

Jack had not been home long when he married Elizabeth Foster, an American girl whose family had moved to Niagara Falls from New York City shortly after her birth in 1861. The McCloys took up residence in a tiny house in the gorge between the Falls and the Whirlpool Rapids. There they established a modest ferrying operation to supplement their income.

In his seasonal work as a tour guide, McCloy had his first glimpses of death at Niagara. On July 8, 1881, Sadie Stewart and Egerton Howie committed suicide together by going over the American Fall after their spouses learned of their torrid romance. McCloy and fellow guide Thomas Conroy pulled Mrs. Stewart's body from the lower river four days later.

Almost from the first, McCloy was attracted to Conroy, possibly because he was much like himself—or what he longed to be. Both were big, strapping Irishmen from Canada with a fierce love of the beauty of the Niagara and an intelligent respect for the river's treachery. But they were a study in contrasts: Conroy was quietly confident and humble; McCloy was brash and ambitious. Conroy was also something McCloy was not: a hero.

In 1874, Conroy had rescued a man from the Canadian Rapids in such dramatic fashion that he became an overnight sensation. New York and Ontario newspapers heralded his feat as though he were a mythic hero of antiquity, but unlike the ancient heroes, Conroy was modest. It is difficult to imagine the awkwardness with which he greeted Simeon Tucker Clark's occasional poem, "Conroy the Brave." published in the June 10, 1874, edition of the *Niagara Falls Gazette*, the lengthy tribute concluded with these ungainly stanzas:

> Strong was the rope that was fast to the shore,
> And under the coil was a heart big and brave—
> Aye, braver today than ever before,

He reaches the rock—and like Perseus of yore—
He rescues his friend from the fiend of the wave!

When the names of our heroes are written or sung,
We will chant your name Conroy in musical stave
When palsied your arm and silent your tongue,
The child now unborn, shall hear how you flung
Yourself in the wave, a comrade to save!

Such a poem, however bad, was just the sort of monument McCloy wanted for himself. He must have been puzzled by Conroy's unwillingness to capitalize on this fame. He likely envied Conroy, but that did not deter him from seeking his company. The two guides forged a friendship that would last many years.

Matthew Webb   *Thomas Conroy*

In 1883, Lizzie McCloy had given birth to Nettie, the girl Captain Webb would kiss before his fatal swim. Jack knew he needed a regular job at good wages to support a family, but he didn't land one until after Webb's death.

In January of that year, the Michigan Central Railway had begun work on a great cantilever bridge at the head of the Whirlpool Rapids. Jack secured a job with one of the bridge labor gangs.

A view down one set of tracks of the Inclined Railway.

The construction of the cantilever bridge utilized a method that would be copied in later years by the builders of Niagara's great arch bridges: work from both sides and meet in the middle. On November 20, 1883, the massive structures erected on opposite banks of the river were no more than a few feet apart. All that remained to complete the span was the placement of several pieces of fabricated steel. The Michigan Central Railway issued instructions that no one was to cross the bridge before or after the gap was joined. The company had reserved the honor of being first to cross for railway Superintendent G. H. Burrows and his wife.

As soon as McCloy received the instruction, he determined to defy it—he was still looking to "make a record" for himself. He found a plank a mere six inches wide, laid it down across the gap in the bridge, and calmly walked from Canada to the United States. The railway fired him for the stunt. Local newspapers made brief mention of it, but it wasn't the kind of record for which he had hoped.

McCloy had always been lucky, and luck carried him through the winter of 1883-84. Not long after he lost his job on the bridge, the Prospect Park Company offered him a full time job as wheelman of the Inclined Railway. McCloy eagerly accepted the position—he knew how to deal with tourists and was suited to the equipment maintenance tasks that went along with the job.

Built in 1843, the Inclined Railway incorporated elements of the elevator and the passenger train to transport visitors from Prospect Park into the gorge to view the American Fall or secure a ferry to Canada. The Railway took its name from the two sets of inclined, parallel rails installed in a deep cut in the gorge face. A trolley-like car rested on each set of rails, connected to its twin by a massive hemp cable that ran around a powered wheel at the top of the gorge. When one car went up the incline, the other came down. It was an elegantly simple mechanism that would have made Archimedes smile.

In 1885, New York State acquired Prospect Park in the process of creating the Niagara Reservation. McCloy stayed on as wheelman. His position entitled him to a modest house in the park where he and his family would live for the better part of two decades. Day after day, McCloy attended to the mundane tasks of greasing machinery and herding passengers, but when there was trouble someone always came looking for him.

1886 was a year of memorable troubles. In March, McCloy led the work crew that recovered the body of L. G. DeWitt from the disintegrating ice mountain facing the American Fall. There was no glory to be had in rescuing the dead, but McCloy contributed to the effort with enthusiasm.

Shortly after 7:00 p.m. on October 5, 1886, 21-year-old Charles Robinson accidentally rowed into the American Rapids, where a rock shattered his boat and pitched him overboard about two hundred feet above Bath Island. The rock that destroyed his boat also provided temporary safety. Protruding from it was an iron rod—a remnant of the Pettibone Paper Mill that had until recently stood on the island. Robinson seized the rod, wrapped his legs around it, and began to scream for help.

Two Reservation police officers heard his cries and reported their discovery to Reservation Superintendent Thomas V. Welch. Welch ordered them to fetch McCloy and Tom Conroy.

Officer Henry Highland found Jack McCloy at home and breathlessly acquainted him with the crisis. When they arrived at Bath Island they were met by Tom Conroy. Conroy had been on duty at the Armory with the 42nd Separate Company, the equivalent of a modern National Guard unit.

Douglas Perry, a laborer familiar with the treacherous waters about Bath Island, volunteered to help McCloy and Conroy. As they scrounged ropes and formulated a rescue plan, hundreds of men from the village gathered to lend assistance.

Gangs of volunteers built huge bonfires on Bath Island and along the shore of Goat

Island to illuminate the rapids as McCloy and Conroy took coils of rope in hand and entered the water. Perry followed, supporting himself with a staff. It was 8:30 p.m. when they began to work their way upstream.

They waded along the submerged ruins of the old paper mill until they were about fifty feet from Robinson's position. Waist-deep in swift water, McCloy and Conroy knew they could move no further in safety. They halted and flung their ropes toward the young man clinging to the iron rod just upriver. Robinson caught one and drew it around the iron rod then let the end float back downstream to his rescuers. The line segments were then drawn tight to form hand holds. Robinson caught another rope and tied it around his waist. He began to move downstream, but he was so exhausted from his ordeal that every step was a battle to maintain his footing. The river urged him ever faster along the ropes until he finally collapsed into the waiting arms of McCloy, Conroy, and Perry. The rescuers took turns carrying him through the rapids, at times passing him like a sack of grain from one man to the next. They did not reach safety until nearly 11:00 p.m.

As the men waded ashore, a jubilant throng of villagers erupted in wild cheering. The bright orange light of the bonfires flickered on the trees and rapids, glistening on the silhouettes of the rescuers and their charge. It was a fairy tale scene that would be recalled vividly for decades.

On October 6, the *Gazette* proclaimed, "If ever men deserved a recognition from the Life-Saving Service, Messrs. McCloy, Conroy, and Perry do. Too much praise cannot be awarded them for their bravery." In 1874 Congress had established the Life-Saving Service, a predecessor of the United States Coast Guard that maintained rescue stations along American rivers and coastal waters. The Service also awarded medals to anyone who conspicuously rescued persons from drowning.

Captain Charles E. Gaskill, commander of the 42nd Separate Company, successfully petitioned Congressman John Weber to secure a medal for Tom Conroy's 1874 rescue and his part in the rescue of Robinson. On June 7, 1887, at the military ball dedicating the 42nd Separate Company's new armory, Weber presented to Conroy a silver medal from the Life-Saving Service.

Perry and McCloy received no honor beyond the local press accounts. McCloy made no public mention of any disappointment he may have felt.

In the afternoon of November 11, 1887, William Glassbrook saw a flock of ducks feeding in the eddies below Goat Island. He set out with his shotgun from the Canadian Maid of the Mist landing in a small boat.

Glassbrook, the son of a Niagara ferryman, was confident enough of his skills to row to the huge rocks at the northern foot of the Horseshoe Fall. There the mist rained down in sheets and the river boiled like a witch's cauldron.

Glassbrook tied up his boat and climbed up onto one of the great rocks. As he waited for an eddy to carry the ducks toward him, the river suddenly tore his boat free of its mooring. The young hunter watched in dismay as the boat capsized and floated downstream. He was stranded below the Horseshoe on a rock almost completely shrouded in cold spray. His clothing was already thoroughly soaked and night would arrive soon enough. By morning he would be dead of exposure.

Glassbrook tried to attract attention by firing his shotgun. When he ran out of shells he shouted until his throat was raw. Luckily, the quirky acoustics of the gorge carried his voice to the Canadian shore. Two men there heard him and raised the alarm.

When the news reached McCloy at the Inclined Railway, he rushed to the stairway leading to the foot of Goat Island. There he met Joel Barlow, the Cave of the Winds guide. They collected rope and a long steel miner's drill from a nearby tool shed, and went to the rocky bank below the Horseshoe Fall.

McCloy saw immediately that the man on the rock would never reach safety unassisted. He quickly considered two rescue options: wade through the white water at the fringe of the Horseshoe's plunge pool, or try to find a boat and row to the stranded man's position before nightfall.

McCloy chose to wade. He tied a rope around himself and handed the loose end to Barlow. With the guide's help, he slipped into the water with the miner's drill firmly in his grasp.

The narrow channel between the shore and the rock was a churning chaos of water that boiled up to McCloy's neck. The drill served as a support and ballast that helped him stand against the conflicting currents. He leaned heavily upon the steel shaft as his feet sought a path along the river bottom.

When McCloy reached Glassbrook's position he wound the rope tightly about the great rock. With Barlow holding the other end, Glassbrook was able to use it as a bridge to wade to safety. He had been on the rock for two hours. McCloy followed with Glassbrook's shotgun a moment later.

McCloy gained considerable notoriety for the daring rescue. The *Gazette* once again called for official recognition of his bravery:

> This is by no means the first time McCloy has risked his life to save that of his fellow man, and the Life-Saving Medal could be no more worthily bestowed by Congress than upon Mr. McCloy.

McCloy himself thought his efforts deserved more than just another mention in the *Gazette*. He consulted attorney Charles Cromley on the matter. Cromley agreed to help get a medal for him, but his efforts did not immediately produce results.

McCloy seemed always to be the first on the scene to recover a body or discover a suicide note. In September of 1889 a young woman named Anna Mead jumped into the American Rapids. Immediately after the suicide McCloy spotted her body below the falls, but it vanished before he could recover it. He would soon find out that it was much better to lose a dead body than a living one.

On January 26, 1891, Reservation Officer Henry Highland caught 20-year-old Karl Stevens trying to cross the bridge to Bath Island after the park had closed for the evening. At about 6:00 p.m., as Highland was escorting him back to the mainland, Stevens leaped over the railing into the rapids. He grabbed an icy projection at the base of one of the bridge piers and saved himself from going over the American Fall.

Highland ran to his residence for a ladder and rope. His son, Harry, went to find Jack McCloy.

McCloy arrived at the bridge twenty minutes later. Stevens was now sitting on the ice below the bridge with his legs dangling in the water.

McCloy, Highland, and several other men lowered the ladder over the side of the bridge several yards from Stevens' position. They could find no safe footing for it, so they tied it to the railing. McCloy fastened a length of rope around his body and climbed down into the darkness.

Stevens sat motionless on the ice with his arms crossed and head hunched forward, oblivious to the crash of ice cakes hurtling toward the gorge.

McCloy stepped from the ladder into water that was only three feet deep, but bitterly cold and swift. He waded slowly across the slick river bottom. Stevens looked up and began to move when McCloy came within arms' length.

"Sit still!" McCloy shouted. "I'll save you!" He took the rope from his waist and moved to loop it around Stevens, but the young man rolled into the dark current and swam to an ice-coated rock.

As McCloy advanced on the new position, Stevens raised his hands over his head and pushed himself backward into the river. He was now in the grasp of the rapids.

McCloy waded back to the ladder and climbed to the bridge as quickly as he could. Then, with Highland and the others, he ran to Luna Island to attempt to intercept the man in the water.

They were too late. Stevens dropped into the gorge just north of the island.

McCloy subsequently learned that Stevens committed suicide out of fear that he would follow four members of his family in the awful, lingering death of pulmonary tuberculosis. McCloy would never forget the maniacal grin on Stevens' face as he splashed backward into the dark water. The mantle of Perseus that he had once so aggressively sought, became a weighty burden on McCloy's shoulders that bitter January night.

After Stevens' death, McCloy's job came to absorb so much of his time and energy that his family life began to suffer. He seemed almost obsessed with the Inclined Railway and the Falls. He no longer talked of "making a record" for himself.

Jack McCloy, circa 1895.

In the evening of October 17, 1892, Jack McCloy was summoned to appear before the Mayor and the Common Council of Niagara Falls, New York. Charles Cromley, the attorney McCloy had once asked to help gain broader recognition for his rescues, had finally succeeded in obtaining a medal for McCloy by appealing to Congressman Thomas Bunting.

Cromley introduced McCloy to the assembled dignitaries and an audience of well-wishers with a brief, but stirring speech. After his remarks, Mayor George W. Wright presented McCloy with the Silver Medal conferred by the United States Life-Saving Service. The room thundered with applause.

McCloy finally had the opportunity to do what Tom Conroy had never done; he could capitalize on his fame by giving an acceptance speech that would establish profitable relationships with the town's most powerful men. All of the things that he might once have considered his due were forgotten, however. His speech consisted of only three sentences:

> While appreciating every kind word, I can only say that my feelings overcome me so that I cannot make fitting answer. Born as I was under a foreign flag, I want you to know that I appreciate my citizenship in this country, the government of which has paid me such high honor in conferring its recognition and medal upon me. I want to thank Mr. Cromley, Mr. Welen, Mr. Bunting, and others for their efforts in getting the medal for me.

The next morning he was back on the job at the Inclined Railway where he would continue as wheelman for seven more years.

In the evening of May 9, 1898, 30-year-old Louis Hoehn jumped from the bridge to Bath Island. Hoehn was a morphine addict, and was likely intoxicated. On the bridge he may have been intent on ending his life, but he changed his mind as soon as he entered the water.

When several women riding along the path around Goat Island heard a man screaming, they looked about and spotted the head and shoulders of Hoehn in the middle of the American Rapids. He was hanging onto a rock with one hand while wiping blood from a head laceration with the other. The women raised the alarm.

Hundreds of people soon crowded the shores of the mainland and nearby islands. A handful of men used ropes and pikes to wade from Luna Island to Robinson Island. They fashioned a rope bridge between the islands, but they had no idea how to approach the man in the water. Hoehn was nearly 300 feet upstream, in one of the worst stretches of white water above the American Fall.

It was after 7:00 p.m. when word reached Jack McCloy at the Inclined Railway. He hurried to Robinson Island. He knew these waters as well as any man, and immediately saw a way to save Hoehn. Time, he knew, was precious, so he tied a rope about his waist, took a pike in hand, and waded into the water.

He had done this sort of thing before: feel with the pike for a foothold on the slimy river bottom, then plant his shoe on that spot and take the next cautious step. With dusk settling on the river he wended his way through the torrent. Minutes seemed like hours as McCloy felt his way over rocks and ledges. Water surged to his neck in places and currents sought to sweep him off his feet, but he finally reached the stranded man.

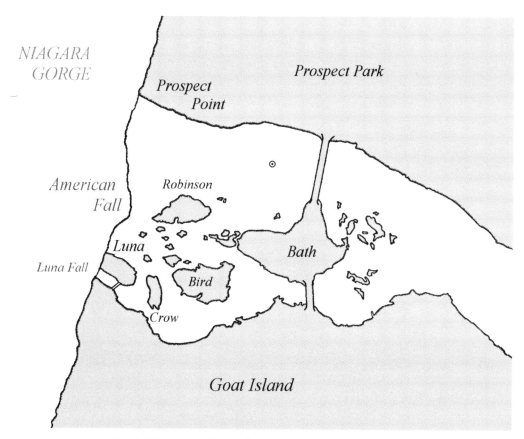

The bullseye marks Hoehn's approximate position
in the rapids above the American Fall.

McCloy pulled the rope taut and unfastened it from himself. He told Hoehn to lift one of his arms.

"I'll try," Hoehn responded. He clung to the rock with one hand while McCloy tied the rope tightly about his midsection.

McCloy startled Hoehn with his next instruction. "Let go!"

Hoehn hesitated for a moment, then did as he had been told. Instantly the current moved him downstream. With increasing rapidity he bounded through the rapids toward the American Fall.

The rescuers on Robinson Island were at first as startled as Hoehn, but they quickly recovered and hauled furiously on the rope. As they did so, Hoehn swept through the rapids in a great arc that carried him hundreds of feet downstream. He came perilously close to dropping into the gorge before the rescue party finally halted his progress and pulled him ashore.

Cheering erupted from the throng of spectators but it slowly faded as all present realized that McCloy was now in the rapids without a life line. All eyes turned to the lonely figure of the wheelman.

McCloy had waited to watch Hoehn's recovery before attempting to save himself. With great care, leaning into the current or on his pike as circumstances dictated, he headed back for Robinson Island. It was exhausting work, but McCloy accomplished it before sunset. He waded ashore to a new round of applause.

The next day the *Buffalo Morning Courier* described McCloy's feat as "one of the most daring rescues from Niagara's torrent ever recorded." Similar praise appeared in other local newspapers. McCloy did not receive, nor did he seek, further recognition for what proved to be his last rescue.

In 1904 McCloy left the Inclined Railway to work as a carpenter with the International Paper Company. No doubt many factors prompted him to leave the job and the place he loved so much. Money certainly played a part, but his departure could not merely have been a quest for higher wages. His old friend Conroy was gone, having become a police constable in 1892, and later a city fireman. McCloy's marriage had been on the rocks for years and ended with a separation due, in part, to his obsession with the river. But his obsession could not overcome the bald fact of his age; he was fifty-three years old. Plunging into the rapids to haul out accident victims and would-be suicides was the work of young men. He had no stomach for losing another Karl Stevens.

Jack McCloy died of a coronary embolism in his hotel room in Niagara Falls, New York, on June 11, 1907. Less than a month after he was buried in Oakwood Cemetery, the huge manila cable of the Inclined Railway snapped. The Railway's twin cars plummeted to the bottom of the gorge, killing one tourist and seriously injuring four others. New York State replaced the Railway with an elevator in 1909.

Lizzie McCloy did not follow her husband in death until 1954. She was buried with him in Oakwood Cemetery, not far from the final resting place of Captain Matthew Webb.

AFTERWORD

I was born upon thy bank, river,
My blood flows in thy stream,
And thou meanderest forever
At the bottom of my dream.

—*Henry David Thoreau*

Niagara Falls has always fascinated and frightened me. It is a place that has been in my dreams since I was a little boy. I grew up in Niagara Falls, New York, but I never paid serious attention to the great cataracts until fairly recently. I was nearly forty years old when I first visited the Cave of the Winds and rode the *Maid of the Mist*. There are thousands of people in Western New York and Southern Ontario who are just like I was: indifferent to these magnificent things so close at hand. It's like having the great Egyptian pyramids in your back yard and never wondering who built them, or why. Well, now that the great cataracts have my attention, I'm obsessed with them. And I'm afraid—not so much for myself—but for those people who don't know what they mean or what they can do.

About two miles above the falls there are signs warning boaters to proceed no further downriver, yet every summer fishermen and pleasure boaters journey well beyond these signs. Every summer at least one fool wades into the rapids from Luna Island or the Three Sisters to grope in the rushing water for pocket change thrown away for luck by tourists. Every year, in all seasons, suicides wade into the rapids from Table Rock or Prospect Point, thinking, perhaps, that dying in such a lovely place will be a pleasant experience. They are mistaken.

As a boy I did many foolish and reckless things, but none more so than to swim in the upper Niagara. On blazing summer days my friends and I would scale the concrete piers that support the east span of the North Grand Island Bridges. We would cross along the utility catwalk from LaSalle to Buckhorn Island. I can still hear the roar of Thruway traffic overhead and the shrill cries of gulls soaring beneath us.

At the third pier out from Buckhorn we clambered down to the steel arch beneath the roadway. From there we stepped out into the humid breeze and plummeted thirty feet to the cool, green water flowing inexorably toward the Falls. It was exhilarating. The current in that part of the river runs to perhaps four miles per hour. By the time we surfaced after a plunge we would be halfway downstream to the west span and the massive steel plates buttressing the bridge piers against the river. Then we would swim back.

Again and again we would climb up a makeshift ladder to the arch to jump—until we were exhausted from swimming and climbing. It was as exciting as any amusement park ride, but far more dangerous. I suppose we were emboldened by stories of older boys who had survived inner tube runs through the rapids at Devil's Hole. We were as blithely ignorant of our peril as they. The Niagara is an unforgiving river, but we didn't know that—or didn't care. It was summer and we were boys.

We were not content to exercise our foolishness four miles above the Falls; in spring and summer we splashed into the shallow rapids at the head of Celinda Eliza Island, less than half a mile above the Horseshoe. Sometimes we sat on a flat rock and dangled our legs in the swift channel between Celinda Eliza and Solon Island. Had I known then what I now know, I would not have been so carefree, so oblivious.

Over the past two centuries only a small number of children have gone over the Falls or drowned in the rapids that surge through the gorge. I have odd, oblique associations with three of them. I went to school with the boys who were with Mark Zebrowsky the day he disappeared on an ice floe above the Horseshoe in April 1967. My older brother was at the time a classmate of Mark's older brother. In 1970, David Fenitz, my best friend's cousin, went over the American Fall on a makeshift raft. I had hoped David was the last boy to die in this awful fashion, but he was not.

In the afternoon of April 13, 1998, I was driving along the river on my way to the Niagara Falls Public Library to research a story. It was warm and sunny. The sky was a brilliant July blue, but the sun was too low in the sky for the hour, and the trees too bare for anyone to mistake it for a summer afternoon.

I always take the river route to the library. I like to watch for boats in the prohibited zone above the Falls and ask myself, "Who is stupid today?" There were no boats on the water that Monday afternoon, even though the winter had been mild and the river was free of pack ice. I looked for them anyway, and listened to the radio as I drove. As I neared my exit, not far from Goat Island, the hourly news came on. The lead story was that of a boy who had fallen into the American Rapids. A search was underway. Helicopters and the Swift Water Rescue Team were at the scene. My heart raced as the import of the radio broadcast seeped into my daydreams: I, too, was at the scene.

I wanted to drive to Goat Island and join the search, but I did not. I knew that the river would be finished with the boy by the time I got there. I also knew that I would probably just have distracted or impeded the men who know how to rescue people. I drove to the library instead, hoping all the way that the story was a false alarm, that the missing boy had been rescued, or merely wandered off and was found.

But it had not been a false alarm. Six-year-old Richard Karm of Buffalo died that day. He had been on an outing organized by Community Services for the Developmentally Disabled. The group, which included Richard's mother and her boyfriend, visited the Niagara Falls Aquarium before going to the Niagara Reservation for a picnic. While on Green Island, several adults noticed Richard playing near the water's edge. As they ran toward him to bring him away from danger, he somehow fell in.

The rapids around Green Island are very shallow, but swift. An adult would have little trouble wading through them, but the river bottom there is slick with moss and algae. John Asklar, a fireman who waded through those rapids looking for Richard that day, later said, "It was like walking on grease."

There was nothing anyone could do, really. The shallow rapids carried Richard into deeper, swifter water. His mother's boyfriend, 35-year-old Richard Rowe, made a valiant effort to rescue the boy, but it was too late. Richard Karm vanished. Several days later I learned that my friend's wife, a physical therapist, had treated the boy.

When I saw his photograph in the *Buffalo News*, I thought of my mother. I know how much she worried about me when I was a boy. I can imagine the horror and anguish she would have felt had I suffered a similar fate. As of this writing Richard Karm's body has not been recovered.

It may be statistically insignificant to have had such tenuous connections to three dead boys, but I still find it oddly disturbing. It would be stranger, I suppose, if I had no connections to victims of the Falls. As the years pass, I find more and more of the dead who are somehow connected to me or my family. The older sister of a boy who grew up just around the corner from me jumped over the Falls. Her body surfaced in Lake Ontario. The young wife of my father's doctor committed suicide at the American Fall.

A witty, perceptive, and talented acquaintance of mine disappeared several years ago after a long battle with drugs and alcohol. He abandoned his home, car, and family immediately after being discharged from the psychiatric wing of Niagara Falls Memorial Medical Center. A mutual friend confided to me that he had likely taken "the big dive"—meaning he had gone over the American Fall. He is still missing.

E. R. Baxter III, one of four great teachers I have known, lost a promising student in the Niagara Gorge in March of 1989, when 25-year-old Edward Mims leaped to his death from the Whirlpool Rapids Bridge. Mims had been trying to cross the border from the United States to visit a friend when Canadian customs officials detained him on suspicion of drug possession. They handed him over to their American counterparts, who released him shortly afterward without pressing charges. For some unknown reason, Mims began walking back across the bridge toward Canada. An American customs agent ran after him. Inexplicably, when Mims saw his pursuer he climbed the railing and jumped. He struck a bridge abutment and tumbled to the rocks two hundred feet below.

"Ed was an intelligent, talented young man," Baxter said at the time, "and I'm going to miss him." Baxter, a fine poet and essayist, knew talent when he saw it. Several of Mims' poems had appeared in his college literary journal the previous year. They were, as Baxter might say, "good stuff." In "Invitation to an Esoteric Romance," Mims wrote:

> Come with me,
> listen to our footsteps
> And I know by the shifting lights in the long corridors
> behind your eyes
> that you sense the gentle roar of the rapids coming nearer.
> And I want to go off somewhere far where no one can find us.

His poem "On City's Edge" concludes with this stanza:

> On edge of city
> Balance feet
> Relax hands
> Smile face to calm
> The body
> Turn
> Look backwards
> Feel the cool
> Baptismal spray
> The breath of misty
> Sage Niagarans
> Softly thundering upwards
> In me
> Resuscitating
> A dying dream
> I jump inward
> Hoping
> Someone
> Would catch me
> In midair . . .

Good stuff, indeed. I want to read more of Ed Mims' poetry, but there won't be any. His death was ruled a suicide, and his poems were used as evidence against him. I don't know why Mims fled when he had no need to, nor do I know why he jumped from the bridge.

To this day, Baxter doesn't believe Mims killed himself. He thinks Mims was afraid, panicked. Frightened people do stupid things. Like jumping over bridge railings in darkness thinking they are only ten or fifteen feet from the ground. Ten or fifteen feet from the uniform chasing them. Who knows?

My wife and I took the kids to the Great Gorge Trip in Canada several years ago while I was researching my first Niagara Falls book. I remember that as we entered the elevator car that would take us down to the catwalk along the Whirlpool Rapids an excited tourist announced that someone had just jumped from the Rainbow Bridge. Once at the bottom, all I could do was stare at the great green waves that rolled by, looking for a corpse. I saw nothing but great green waves rolling by. The next day I read the details of the suicide in the *Buffalo News*.

I stopped at the Customs Inspection Station at the American end of the Whirlpool Rapids Bridge one day in 1997. I had just come from the Niagara Falls, Ontario, Public Library researching this book. A police cruiser roared up as I stopped my car. A patrolman sprang out and scrambled down the embankment flanking the bridge. I asked the inspector in the booth what was going on. "Someone spotted a body in the river," he said.

On July 13, 1998, I was hiking in the gorge with my son, Teddy, while the body of Jeffrey Williams floated in the Whirlpool. We were there, oblivious, on the American side when the body of the ax murderer was hauled from the water in Canada. We didn't learn about it until we got home that evening.

I have been personally acquainted with only two of Niagara's victims, but there is a skein of death at this place that certainly entangles me. Still, I feel safe. I have grown cautious with age. Like Carlisle Graham, I will one day wear a life preserver whenever I go near the water.

When I consider the thousands who have taken the plunge at Niagara in the past two centuries, I wonder how my friends and I escaped being counted among those lost souls. Those friends are gone now, living separate lives in futures none of us imagined, but I still go down to the river. I visit the Falls as often as I can, though I no longer wade, and swimming is far from my mind. I now find it difficult even to approach the railing at Prospect Point or Luna Island. I am almost afraid to look into the abyss these days. Perhaps it is a late-blossoming fear of heights. Perhaps it is a secret horror that I will hear the voice of the demon that has impelled so many to jump into the mad water.

One day I will no longer be able to visit the place at all. But others will go in my stead. Ignorant boys will swim and wade and blunder into eternity. Drunken boaters will plow into the Canadian rapids and perish at the Horseshoe. The daredevils will come—as they always have come—to "conquer" the Horseshoe. The suicides will heed the demon's call and they, too, will come—to Terrapin Point or Table Rock or Luna Island to jump to their doom.

A multitude will come and die, and the great green river will tumble unceasing into the Niagara Gorge, indifferent to the unending stream of human tragedies.

—T. W. Kriner
March 31, 1999

CHRONOLOGY OF NIAGARA STUNTS

1829

October 7-17
Sam Patch performed a series of dives from a platform towering ninety feet over the lower river at the foot of Goat Island.

1859

June 30 - September 8
Funambulist Jean François Gravelet, also known as "Blondin" or the "Prince of Manila," repeatedly walked a tightrope across the Niagara Gorge.

1860

June 6 - September 15
Blondin performed his second series of tightrope walks across the gorge.

August 15 - September 20
William Leonard Hunt, billing himself as Guillermo Antonio Farini, duplicated Blondin's performances.

1865

June 15
Harry Leslie walked across the gorge on a tightrope.

1869

August 25
J. F. "Professor" Jenkins crossed the gorge on a tightrope.

1873

August 25 - September 10
Henry Balleni, billing himself as "The Great Australian Blondin," crossed the gorge on a tightrope and performed many stunts, including an early demonstration of bunjee jumping.

September 10
Stephen Peer, an assistant to Henry Balleni, crossed the gorge on his employer's rope.

1874

July 27
Stephen Peer duplicated his feat.

1876

July 8 - 27
Maria Spelterini made numerous crossings of the gorge on a tightrope, including several with her feet in peach baskets.

1879

May 28
Henry Peer, a cousin of Stephen Peer, leaped from the Upper Suspension Bridge.

1883

July 24
Captain Matthew Webb died attempting to swim the Whirlpool Rapids without a life preserver.

1886

July 11
Carlisle Graham rode a barrel through the Whirlpool Rapids.

August 8
William Potts and George Hazlett together traversed the Whirlpool Rapids in a single barrel.

August 19
Carlisle Graham made his second barrel trip through the Whirlpool Rapids

August 22
William Kendall, wearing a life preserver, swam the Whirlpool Rapids.

August 24
James Scott died attempting to swim the Devil's Hole Rapids.

November 7
Lawrence Donovan jumped from the Upper Suspension Bridge.

November 28
George Hazlett made his second barrel run through the Whirlpool Rapids, this time accompanied by Sadie Allen.

1887

June 15
Carlisle Graham rode his barrel through the Whirlpool Rapids for the third time.

June 22
Stephen Peer returned to Niagara for his third crossing of the gorge on a tightrope.

June 25
Stephen Peer died upon falling from his tightrope in an attempt to cross the Niagara Gorge. Peer had evidently been drinking before mounting the rope in ordinary hard-soled shoes.

August 28
Charles Percy traversed the Whirlpool in an experimental lifeboat.

1888

July 4
Robert Flack died attempting to ride a boat through the Whirlpool Rapids.

September 16
Charles Percy made his second run through the Whirlpool Rapids in a boat.

1889

August 24
Carlisle Graham rode his barrel through the Whirlpool Rapids for the fourth time.

September 15
Robert Campbell piloted a boat through the Whirlpool Rapids.

1890

May 3
I. Athey rappelled from the Upper Suspension Bridge to a waiting boat by means of an aluminum tape paid out from a clutch-controlled drum.

September 6
Samuel Dixon crossed the Niagara Gorge on the tightrope left behind by Stephen Peer.

1891
July 17
Samuel Dixon repeated his gorge crossing performance.

1892

October 12
Clifford Calverly performed numerous stunts while making repeated crossings of the gorge on a tightrope.

1893

July 1 - 4
Clifford Calverly returned to give several funambulistic exhibitions and perform a variety of stunts on a cable spanning the gorge.

1896

July 1
James Hardy crossed the Niagara Gorge on a tightrope in a "private" performance.

July 4
James Hardy gave a public exhibition of his funambulistic skills.

1898

June 13
Bobby Leach ran the Whirlpool Rapids in a barrel.

June 19
Bobby Leach made his second barrel run through the gorge.

1900

July 9
Peter Nissen piloted a boat through the Whirlpool Rapids.

1901

September 6
Martha Wagenfurher rode a barrel through the Whirlpool Rapids.

September 7
Maud Willard died in the Whirlpool after a successful barrel ride through the Whirlpool Rapids.

October 12
Peter Nissen ran the Whirlpool Rapids in a boat.

October 13
Peter Nissen traversed the Whirlpool Rapids a second time.

October 24
Annie Edson Taylor plunged over the Horseshoe Fall in a barrel, suffering only minor injuries.

1908

July 1
Bobby Leach descended from the Upper Steel Arch Bridge by means of a parachute.

1910

September 18
Captain Klaus Larsen ran the Whirlpool Rapids in boat.

September 24
Bobby Leach rode a barrel through the Whirlpool Rapids.

1911

June 27
Oscar Williams crossed the Niagara Gorge on a tightrope.

June 28
Bobby Leach once again ran the Whirlpool Rapids in a barrel.

July 25
Bobby Leach became the first man to plunge over the Horseshoe Fall in a barrel.

October 24
Peter Langaard piloted a boat through the Whirlpool Rapids.

October 28
Captain Klaus Larsen returned for his second boat trip through the Whirlpool Rapids.

October 29
Captain Klaus Larsen took his final boat trip through the Whirlpool Rapids.

1920

July 11
Charles Stephens died when his barrel imploded after plunging over the Horseshoe Fall.

1927

September 15
Vincent Taylor made a parachute jump from the Upper Steel Arch Bridge.

1928

July 4
Jean Lussier plunged over the Horseshoe Fall in a sphere constructed of steel, canvas, and rubber.

1930

May 30
William "Red" Hill Sr. traversed the Whirlpool Rapids in a steel cylinder.

July 4
George Stathakis died after plummeting over the Horseshoe Fall in a barrel.

1931

May 31
William "Red" Hill Sr. rode George Stathakis's barrel through the Whirlpool Rapids.

1945

July 8
William "Red" Hill Jr. rode the Stathakis death barrel through the Whirlpool Rapids.

1948

September 1
William "Red" Hill Jr. ran the Whirlpool Rapids in a boat.

1949

July 30
Major Lloyd Hill (son of William and brother of William Jr.) rode through the Whirlpool Rapids in a steel cylinder.

1950

August 6
Major Lloyd Hill made a second trip through the Whirlpool Rapids in a steel cylinder.

1951

August 5
William "Red" Hill Jr. died upon plunging over the Horseshoe Fall in a cylinder made of netting and truck tire innertubes.

1954

July 31
Major Lloyd Hill made yet another barrel run through the Whirlpool Rapids.

1956

July 30
Major Lloyd Hill took his last trip through the Whirlpool Rapids.

1961

July 15
William Fitzgerald, also known as Nathan Boya, plunged over the Horseshoe Fall in a steel and rubber sphere.

July 23
Ray Weaver ran the Whirlpool Rapids in a boat.

1975

July 4
Jim Sarten rode a raft through the Whirlpool Rapids in connection with a television production.

1977

June 11
Karel Soucek rode a barrel through the Whirlpool Rapids.

October 31
Kenneth Lagergren piloted a kayak through the Whirlpool Rapids.

1981

October 14
Kenneth Lagergren, Chris Spelius, Don Weedon, and Carrie Ashton traversed the Whirlpool Rapids in kayaks.

1984

July 3
Karel Soucek plunged over the Horseshoe Fall in a steel cylinder.

1985

August 19
Steven Trotter dropped over the Horseshoe Fall in a cylinder made of plastic barrels.

October 5
John David Munday survived a plunge over the Horseshoe in a plastic tank.

1987

October 13
John David Munday made a barrel run through the Whirlpool Rapids.

1988

September 27
Peter DeBernardi and Jeffrey Petkovich made the first duet plunge over the Horseshoe.

1990

June 5
Jessie Sharp died after plummeting over the Horseshoe Fall in a kayak.

1995

June 18
Steven Trotter and Lori Martin made the second duet trip over the Horseshoe Fall.

October 1
Robert Overacker died attempting to conquer the Horseshoe Fall with a jet ski and a parachute.

BIBLIOGRAPHY

Books

Aug, Lisa. *Beyond the Falls: A Modern History of the Lower Niagara River*. Niagara Falls, N. Y.: Niagara Books, 1992.

Berton, Pierre. *Niagara: A History of the Falls*. Toronto: McClelland and Stewart, 1994.

Devoy, John. *A History of the City of Buffalo and Niagara Falls*. Buffalo, N. Y.: The Times, 1896.

Dow, Charles Mason. *Anthology and Bibliography of Niagara Falls*. Albany: State of New York, 1921.

Dumych, Daniel. *Niagara Falls*. Images of America Series. Charleston: Arcadia Publishing, 1996.

Dumych, Daniel. *Niagara Falls Volume II*. Images of America Series. Charleston: Arcadia Publishing, 1998.

Graham, Lloyd. *Niagara Country*. American Folkways Series. New York: Duell, Sloan, and Pearce, 1949.

Howells, William Dean, et al. *The Niagara Book*. New York: Doubleday, Page, and Company, 1901.

Mizer, Hamilton B. *Niagara Falls, New York: A Selected Topical History of the City's Formative Years*. Lockport, N. Y.: Niagara County Historical Society, 1981.

Palish, Charles Carlin. *Queen of the Mist: The Story of Annie Edson Taylor*. Edited by John W. Percy. Interlaken, N. Y.: Empire State Books, 1987.

Seibel, George A. *Bridges Over the Niagara Gorge*. Edited by Olive M. Seibel. Niagara Falls, Ont.: Niagara Falls Bridge Commission, 1991.

Seibel, George A. *Ontario's Niagara Parks*. Edited by Olive M. Seibel. Niagara Falls, Ont.: Niagara Parks Commission, 1995.

Simpson, Keith. *Forensic Medicine*, 9th ed. London: Edward Arnold, 1985.

Tesmer, Irving H., Ed. *Colossal Cataract: The Geologic History of Niagara Falls*. Albany: State University of New York Press, 1981.

Twenty-Ninth Annual Report of the Commissioners of the State Reservation at Niagara from October 1, 1911 to September 30, 1912. Albany: State of New York, 1913.

Vogel, Michael N. *Echoes in the Mist*. Chatsworth, Cal.: Windsor Publications, 1991.

Wilner, Merton M. *Niagara Frontier: A Narrative and Documentary History*. Chicago: S. J. Clarke, 1931.

Newspapers, Various Issues, 1821-1998

American Courier (Philadelphia)
Buffalo Commercial Advertiser
Buffalo Courier Express
Buffalo Daily Courier
Buffalo Evening News (includes *Buffalo News*)
Buffalo Morning Express
Buffalo Patriot
Buffalo Times
Cataract Journal
Daily Albany Argus
Daily Cataract
Harper's Weekly
Herald-Standard (Uniontown, Pennsylvania)
Lockport Daily Advertiser and Democrat

Niagara Courier (U.S.)
Niagara Falls Gazette (U.S., includes *Niagara Gazette*)
Niagara Falls Journal (U.S.)
Niagara Falls News (U.S.)
Niagara Falls Review (Canada)
New York Herald
New York Times
New York Tribune
St. Catherines Standard
Suspension Bridge Journal

Interviews

Baxter, E. R. III. March 1999.
Joyce, James. July - August 1998.
Zureich, Michael. October - November 1998.
Zureich, Pat. November 1998.

Unpublished Sources

Aiken, Bruce D. "The Great Blondin's Crossings of the Niagara Gorge in 1859." Manuscript from the Local History Collection. Niagara Falls (N. Y.) Public Library, 1999.

Aiken, Bruce D. "The Great Blondin's Crossings of the Niagara Gorge in 1860." Manuscript from the Local History Collection. Niagara Falls (N. Y.) Public Library, 1999.

Dunlap, Orrin E. "Niagara Suicides." Manuscript from the Dunlap Collection, Niagara Falls (N. Y.) Public Library, 1904.

Dunlap, Orrin E. "Schooner Michigan Over the Falls." Manuscript draft and notes from the Dunlap Collection, Niagara Falls (N. Y.) Public Library, circa 1892.

IMAGE CREDITS

Cover - *Under Niagara*, lithograph by Frederic Edwin Church, 1862. Courtesy of the Niagara Falls (N. Y.) Public Library.

pp. 18-25 - from "Miss Ryler's Suicide at Niagara Falls" (artist unknown), Old Franklin Publishing House, Philadelphia, 1886.

pp. 38-44 - Courtesy of Michael Zureich.

pp. 50-55 - Courtesy of James Joyce.

p. 62 - Courtesy of the Niagara Falls (N. Y.) Public Library.

p. 64 - From the September 8, 1889, edition of the *Buffalo Times (artist unknown)*.

p. 73 - Courtesy of the *Niagara Gazette*.

p. 74 - Courtesy of the *Niagara Gazette* (artist unknown).

p. 77 - Courtesy of the Niagara Falls (N. Y.) Public Library.

pp. 80-81 - Courtesy of the *Niagara Gazette*.

pp. 84-89 - Courtesy of the Niagara Falls (N. Y.) Public Library.

p. 92 - Courtesy of the *Niagara Gazette*.

pp. 96-197 - Courtesy of the Niagara Falls (N. Y.) Public Library.

ACKNOWLEDGMENTS

I could not have written this book without the help of many fine librarians. I am deeply indebted to those at the the the Niagara Falls (Ont.) Public Library, the Buffalo and Erie County Public Library, E. H. Butler Library (State University College at Buffalo), and the Lockwood Library (State University of New York at Buffalo).

I owe special thanks to Maureen Fennie, Manager of the Local History Department of the Niagara Falls (N.Y.) Public Library. Her enthusiasm and research assistance proved invaluable.

William P. Loos of the Buffalo and Erie County Public Library Rare Book Room provided access to early Buffalo newspapers.

Mary Karen Delmont, Archivist at the E. H. Butler Library, kindly searched the *Courier Express* Collection for photographs and clippings.

James Neiss lent technical assistance in copying photographs from the *Niagara Gazette* archives.

Many thanks are due Don Glynn and the *Niagara Gazette* for their generous support.

I am indebted to Richard Barton, E. R. Baxter III, Patrick Didas, Brenda Evans, Donna Felich-Joyce, Steven Johnson, Joseph Loss, Joyce E. Miller, Daniel M. Romero, and Susan Scheller for their comments on the manuscript.

Greatly appreciated is the research assistance provided by Walter F. Rutkowski, Executive Director of the Carnegie Hero Fund Commission.

Pierre Berton kindly took the time to search his files for news clippings.

Much essential information could not have been obtained without the help of Officer Richard Shaw of the Niagara Falls (N. Y.) Police Department, Niagara County Coroner James M. Joyce, Niagara County Historian Dorothy Rolling, and Sherman Zavitz, Official Historian of Niagara Falls, Ontario.

I am grateful, as always, to Kim for her patience and understanding—and for not pushing me into the river.

INDEX

Notes

In the Canadian Rapids. Visitors to Celinda Eliza Island, circa 1900.

About the Author

T. W. Kriner is a noted Niagara historian. He lives in Williamsville, New York, with his wife, three children, and four cats.

ORDER FORM

IN THE MAD WATER

ISBN 0-9657245-1-4 **$17.95**

JOURNEYS TO THE BRINK OF DOOM

ISBN 0-9657245-0-6 **$14.95**

Sales tax:

Please add state and local taxes for books shipped to New York addresses

Shipping:

Book rate: $2.00 for the first book and 75 cents for each additional book (delivery may take three to four weeks)

First class: $3.00 per book

Payment:

Check or Money Order Only - **DO NOT SEND CASH**

	Price	Qty.	Total
In the Mad Water	$17.95		
Journeys to the Brink of Doom	$14.95		
Book Rate shipping			
First Class shipping			
NYS Sales Tax			
		Total	

Checks payable to:

J & J Publishing
P. O. Box 241
Buffalo, New York 14205
SAN: 299-2795

Ship to:

Name:

Street:

City, State, Zip: